ROUTLEDGE LIBRARY EDITIONS: LIBRARY AND INFORMATION SCIENCE

Volume 51

LIBRARY CRIME AND SECURITY

LIBRARY CRIME AND SECURITY
An International Perspective

ALAN JAY LINCOLN AND
CAROL ZALL LINCOLN

LONDON AND NEW YORK

First published in 1987 by The Haworth Press, Inc.

This edition first published in 2020
by Routledge
2 Park Square, Milton Park, Abingdon, Oxon OX14 4RN

and by Routledge
52 Vanderbilt Avenue, New York, NY 10017

Routledge is an imprint of the Taylor & Francis Group, an informa business

© 1987 The Haworth Press, Inc.

All rights reserved. No part of this book may be reprinted or reproduced or utilised in any form or by any electronic, mechanical, or other means, now known or hereafter invented, including photocopying and recording, or in any information storage or retrieval system, without permission in writing from the publishers.

Trademark notice: Product or corporate names may be trademarks or registered trademarks, and are used only for identification and explanation without intent to infringe.

British Library Cataloguing in Publication Data
A catalogue record for this book is available from the British Library

ISBN: 978-0-367-34616-4 (Set)
ISBN: 978-0-429-34352-0 (Set) (ebk)
ISBN: 978-0-367-42580-7 (Volume 51) (hbk)
ISBN: 978-0-367-42584-5 (Volume 51) (pbk)
ISBN: 978-0-367-85366-2 (Volume 51) (ebk)

Publisher's Note
The publisher has gone to great lengths to ensure the quality of this reprint but points out that some imperfections in the original copies may be apparent.

Disclaimer
The publisher has made every effort to trace copyright holders and would welcome correspondence from those they have been unable to trace.

Library Crime and Security: An International Perspective

Alan Jay Lincoln
Carol Zall Lincoln

The Haworth Press
New York • London

Library Crime and Security: An International Perspective has also been published as *Library & Archival Security*, Volume 8, Numbers 1/2, Spring/Summer 1986.

© 1987 by The Haworth Press, Inc. All rights reserved. No part of this work may be reproduced or utilized in any form or by any means, electronic or mechanical, including photocopying, microfilm and recording, or by any other information storage and retrieval system, without permission in writing from the publisher. Printed in the United States of America.

Haworth Press, Inc., 12 West 32 Street, New York, NY 10001
EUROSPAN/Haworth, 3 Henrietta Street, London, WC2E 8LU England

Library of Congress Cataloging-in-Publication Data

Library crime and security.

"Library crime and security: an international perspective has also been published as Library & archival security, volume 8, nos. 1/2, spring/summer 1986"—T.p. verso.
  Bibliography: p.
  Includes index.
  1. Libraries—Securities measures. 2. Book thefts—Prevention. 3. Books—Mutilation, defacement, etc.—Prevention. 4. Crime and criminals. I. Lincoln, Alan Jay. II. Lincoln, Carol Zall.
Z679.6.L49   1987   025.8'2   87-12059
ISBN 0-86656-480-2

Library Crime and Security: An International Perspective

Library & Archival Security
Volume 8, Numbers 1/2

CONTENTS

Preface	xi
Chapter One: Libraries and Crime: A Comparative View	1
Chapter Two: Library Crime in Great Britain	19
Chapter Three: Library Crime in Canada	59
Chapter Four: Three Studies of Library Crime	89
Chapter Five: Patterns of Library Security	115
Chapter Six: Controlling Crime: A Security Checklist	145
Bibliography	153
Index	155

Preface

The problems of crime and disruption in libraries are not new. It is likely that the earliest libraries took precautions to protect their valuable contents. Chaining books to tables, although cumbersome, was effective. Today there are continuing problems with the theft of resources as well as concerns about damage to property and the safety of those using the library for legitimate purposes. The techniques that have been developed to prevent and control crime are far more sophisticated than the chaining of books. It is our hope that in the presentation of research about library crime and disruption in five countries, we can provide insights into the problems faced by librarians and stimulate thought about the range of solutions to the problem of crime and disruption.

What is included. The focus is on the patterns of library crime and disruption in Great Britain, Canada and the United States. In addition to a good deal of data on these problems there is extensive information on the characteristics of the institutions and the communities in which they are found. The relationships between these characteristics and the patterns of crime is a major concern. It is important to understand not only the patterns of crime but how crime affects our lives. Thus, the impact of crime on the institution and the individual is examined. This includes analysis of the responses to crime in the form of security options used in public libraries. Finally, an extensive security checklist is developed that may serve as a guide for making the library a safer and more secure setting for staff, patrons and contents.

What is not included. There have been several extensive reviews of the literature on library crime and security published in recent years. We felt that the reader would gain little by seeing these studies one more time. We also did not attempt to develop complicated crime prevention programs that could be adopted by the local library. Once again, detailed treatments of these programs can be found in several recent publications. Both the reviews and selected security publications are cited in Chapter six for the reader who would like to pursue these in more detail.

There are several people whom we would like to single out for their help on this project. Peter Mann and the Centre for Library and Information Management in Loughborough, England, provided the support necessary for the study of Great Britain. Peter Gellatly of The Haworth Press encouraged us to complete the work when the task appeared to be overwhelming. Students in the Criminal Justice Research Seminar at the University of Lowell provided valuable assistance in the preparation of data and offered many useful suggestions. We would not have reliable studies without the thousands of librarians who took the time to complete our survey instruments and provide the insightful comments that are scattered throughout the text. Their statements provide an additional level of understanding of the problems of crime and disruption. Harriet Lincoln carefully read major portions of the manuscript and provided valuable suggestions. Alisa and Debra, two independent young women, made sure that we had the time to devote to the preparation of this volume. To all we are grateful.

Chapter One

Libraries and Crime: A Comparative View

INTRODUCTION

The field of library science has been changing in the last two decades. Some of the changes have resulted from innovations in technology; others have come about in response to changing needs of the community and of patrons. Advances in information storage and retrieval have enabled libraries to provide more varied information in less time, but have also strained the budgets of many libraries. Shifting centers and characteristics of the population have forced some public libraries to expand and modify services at a rapid rate, while other libraries have seen declines in the number of patrons.

Many of these issues extend beyond the control of the public library. Public libraries in the United States have been described in the following way: "As the public library approached the last quarter of the 20th century it was beset with a number of difficult problems. The principal one continued to be that of adequate financial support. Urban libraries, particularly those in the older cities of the Northeast and Midwest, were suffering from the effects of urban blight, the flight to the suburbs, and sharply increasing expenses of operation." (Encyclopedia of Library and Information Science, 1976:288). While this was written about U.S. libraries, the same issues are having an impact in Great Britain and Canada. Economic problems at a national or local level may be manifested in budget cutbacks for libraries and library systems. When cutbacks or even stabilizations occur, they affect both the functioning of the library and the patrons they serve. Present restrictions are particularly inopportune because libraries are undergoing technological changes that often entail great expense. For example, a choice may have to be made between maintaining the current level of acquisitions or adding database information systems. To adapt to the changing habits of the population, many libraries now provide videotapes, audiotapes and computer discs. The effects of these technological changes can be seen beyond the level of the local library. Many graduate programs have maintained a modern image by changing their program titles to include "information science."

Other changes in the community may have an impact upon the public library. The growing trend to deinstitutionalize the mentally ill affects public institutions. Unless adequate support services are provided for ex-hospital residents, many staying on the streets seek shelter in safe and warm places. Unfortunately, as has been shown in countless communities, the public library meets these needs. Furthermore, changes in the structure of the family and employment patterns may be leading to more unsupervised time for children. Rather than return to an empty home after school, these children may stay on the streets or make use of whatever public facilities are available.

The shifting of population patterns through migration and immigration may require the library to reassess the services provided to the community. Popular and special interest materials may have to be ordered in more than one language. For example, some urban United States libraries have dramatically increased their expenditure on materials in Spanish. Similarly, some British libraries are providing increased materials for the Indian, Pakistani, Middle Eastern and other groups in the population. Canadian libraries are mandated to provide appropriate materials for a variety of ethnic groups found within the area they serve. Immigrants are not the only segment of the population requiring specialized service. Demographic changes such as the increasing proportion of elderly may place special demands on selected library services. The impact of these social changes on the library will be magnified if crime and disruption also become a significant problem.

One of the disturbing changes in industrialized nations has been the significant increase in crime. As will be shown in greater detail in later chapters, each of the countries studied in this project has experienced increases in crime. It may be that in addition to all the other potential problems faced by libraries, the occurrence and threat of crime is among the most difficult to manage. This is in part due to the fact that many of the causes and factors perpetuating crime are beyond the control of the library or librarian. For example, high rates of unemployment influence the crime rate in a community. While it is true that the library may face increased demand for services by those who find themselves out of work, the increased rate of crime in the community will probably not be affected by anything that the library does or does not do. However, the library does not exist separately from the community and its problems. If there is an increase in crime as a result of unemployment or some other social issue such as ethnic or racial tension, then the library may suffer along with other public and private institutions.

Some types of crime are easier to control and prevent than others. For example, while librarians may have some success in reducing theft and vandalism, it is much more difficult to control some of the more violent crimes carried out by determined individuals. As pointed out by Camp (*ALA Yearbook*, 1985:259): "The shooting of President Reagan, President Ford's two near misses, the assassination of President Kennedy demonstrate rather conclusively that dozens of guards are unable to protect even a President against a sociopath with a gun. Referring to the shooting in Cleveland Public [Library], Police chief William Hamton is quoted as saying that 'you can have 1,000 policemen nearby and still not prevent something like that'." Fortunately, deadly attacks within libraries are relatively infrequent.

In the remaining sections of this chapter we will provide brief overviews of: the role of research; a capsule description of the development and "missions" of public libraries in Great Britain, Canada and the United States; and a summary of the risk factors most likely to affect public libraries.

FUNCTIONS OF RESEARCH

It is natural to try to understand the world around us. We tend to ask about the things that intrigue, interest and affect us most. For example, if we make our living by fishing, then we tend to be curious about the best ways to bring in the largest catch. We might base our opinions on any number of possible factors, including tradition or folklore, a single personal experience, the reports of others or a series of trial and error episodes. But what would happen if the single personal experience happened to be misleading or open to conflicting interpretations? To illustrate, assume that a successful catch occurred early one rainy morning in August in a particular spot. What do we know? Was the catch successful because it was "early morning," "rainy," "in August," or "in a particular spot?" The techniques of everyday observation do not always provide the obvious answers to our vital questions. We may be tempted to overgeneralize about the conditions favoring large catches or to attribute the cause of our success to the wrong critical factor. Eventually, those explanations that tend to work best would be the ones we hold onto. Those that did not work for us would be discarded. Other fishermen would be likely to test our suggestions against their personal experiences and then reject or adopt these "theories" for maximizing the catch. Similarly, we might be concerned about the factors that increase or reduce the amount of book theft in a library. Research often is initiated as we seek answers to important, everyday questions.

Scientific research protects us from making the common mistakes of every day inquiry. The use of controlled and systematic observation is a crucial factor in scientific inquiry. This is true whether we are studying conditions that increase the catch of fish, causes of a contagious disease, conditions that facilitate theft, or characteristics of the typical mystery reader. Scientific research can be used for many purposes. A recent British Public Libraries Research Group Workshop focused on the role of in-house research in public libraries. In the preface to that report, Linda Stewart (1984) suggested that the "main value of research lies in the guidance that it gives to action." She goes on to identify four kinds of research that can be helpful in solving problems in the library:

- Diagnostic research is primarily intended to supplement information available at the initial stages of problem-solving.
- Comparative research can help in the middle stages of problem-solving when the nature of the problem is fairly clear and there is uncertainty over the range of solutions available and/or likely consequences of adopting alternate solutions.
- Evaluative research is concerned with the latter stages of problem-solving, i.e., evaluating the outcome of solutions which an organization has selected and implemented.
- Action research—here the researcher plays an active part in all stages of problem-solving. (Stewart, 1984:1)

The major focus of this volume is on comparative victimization studies of crime in public libraries. Victimization studies gather information directly from people who are likely to know about crime affecting them or the institution they are affiliated with. The studies do not rely upon official reports of crime. While the information is first presented in a descriptive manner, the relationships between institutional/community factors and library crime patterns subsequently are presented. It is hoped that the findings answer many of the obvious research questions and that they can be used to develop a variety of programs designed to control crime in the local library setting.

LIBRARY DEVELOPMENT

Great Britain

The concept of the public library as we know it today started in England. Parish, subscription and mercantile libraries were some of the earliest libraries. By the end of the 15th century, Oxford and Cambridge Universities had functioning libraries. Before 1600, Thomas Bodley had established a private library in Oxford. Libraries in Great Britain in the 16th and 17th centuries typically were owned either by corporations or individuals. None was supported by the authorities or the public. According to Albert Predeek's history of libraries in Great Britain, this pattern continued for many years.

> Before the middle of the nineteenth century England had no libraries open to the general public such as the German cities had founded after the Reformation. Likewise the English grammar schools of the sixteenth century and the public schools which sprang from them in the seventeenth and eighteenth centuries, founded with quite considerable libraries, were separated from the people by a much broader gap that has ever been the case with the German Ratschulen and classical Gymnasia. . . . On the other hand, many church and parsonage libraries which were intended for the lower clergy revealed as early as the seventeenth and eighteenth centuries a notable trend toward providing ministers' families with better reading matter and thereby instruction which the common schools could not give. (Predeek, 1947:52)

In 1850 the first public library act was passed. "The Act permitted councils of towns of 10,000 population with the approval of 2/3 majority of the local government electors to provide a building, light, and fuel and employ a librarian at an annual cost not to exceed a halfpenny rate. No provision was made for the purchase of books on the assumption that they would be donated by benefactors" (Phillips, 1977). In 1882 Nottingham established the first children's library. Public libraries grew quickly in England, and by 1900 there were over 350. Many services were common at the libraries. In addition to providing scholarly works, there was an emphasis on adult education. Newspaper areas as well as children's areas were available. The rural areas were helped by the Carnegie United Kingdom Trust with funds for the initial construction of libraries.

In the 1920s the Kenyon committee prepared a report on libraries in England and Wales. This committee was charged with determining the adequacy of library services. While no legislation followed, a general theme of cooperation did result. In 1959 the Roberts Report, which was to study the structure of public library service in England and Wales, became a guide for future patterns of reorganization. The Bourdillon Report of 1962 also had a strong impact on the British library system. This report set the standards for public library service in both England and Wales. Using the recommendations from the Roberts Report concerning the basic requirements of an efficient library, The Bourdillon Report detailed the standards for staffing, basic library service, building and other services. For example, one standard for basic library service was:

> A library providing a basic library service should purchase annually the following library materials: (a) for lending purposes, not less than 2,000 titles of adult non-fiction from the new and older British publications, American and other English language publications from abroad and music scores; together with 300 volumes to allow for duplicates and replacements. (Phillips, 1977:Section 33)

In 1964 the Public Libraries and Museum Act reorganized previous legislation and revised the structure of libraries in Great Britain. This act drew from both the Roberts Report and the Bourdillon Report. "This act designated library authorities covering the whole of England and Wales, allocated to each the duty to provide a comprehensive and efficient library service . . . ." (Jones and Sewell, 1976:150). In 1972 the British Library Act officially regrouped the British libraries into three separate divisions including reference, lending, and bibliographic services. This act functioned to centralize several different services including mobile library service, school library service, hospital library service, service to the aged and housebound, prison service and service to the army. The British Library became the hub of the British library system rather than the apex. According to Hookway, the hub ". . . should be more sensitive and quickly responsive to problems and needs elsewhere" (1976:43). Hookway continued by describing the future of the British library system.

> Library and information services are under increasing pressure to satisfy from limited resources a wide range of educational, recreational, scholarly, industrial, commercial and other needs. Individual libraries and information services are never likely to meet all the demands of a modern society, and yet as much information as needed should be made available throughout the U.K. as rapidly as necessary and in the most useful and economic form. (1976:44)

As of April, 1974, the 385 previous library authorities were replaced by 117 newly aligned library authorities. The new districts were based on population areas from a minimum of at least 100,000 to over 1,000,000. According to Wilson (1976:202), "Coordination of all publicly supported library services will take place at local level, linked with the service of the British Library to create a truly national library and information service."

Canada

> The history of Canadian Libraries parallels to some extent that of the U.S. but there are also many differences. First there are the French origins of eastern Canada and the continued domination of the French language and culture in Quebec. Then, there is the long colonial status of Canada and the close cultural and political ties with Great Britain, even after the achievement of Dominion and Commonwealth status. Finally, there are the vast distances, the sparse population, the slow development of transportation, and the long winters that accentuate the difficulties in socialization and communication. Despite the difficulties, the development of Canadian libraries has been steady and today they are in much the same position as those of Europe and the United States. (Johnson and Harris, 1976:216)

Canada is a "multicultural society" or a mosaic. Less than half the population is descended from immigrants from the British Isles. An additional 25-30% of Canadians are of French origin, while about a fourth are other European in background. The largest of these latter groups include German, Italian, Ukrainian and Dutch. Native populations and small proportions of Asians complete the mosaic. In order to accommodate the cultural backgrounds of its population, the Canadian library has to provide books, periodicals and newspapers that are published in 30 languages.

The earliest libraries typically were those developed by individuals, religious orders and government agencies. Prior to the British takeover in the 1760s, nearly all available books were in the private collections of priests or government officials. Public or subscription libraries first appeared about 1800 in what is now Ontario. The first mechanics' institute was created in 1827 in Newfoundland. In 1851 Parliament legislated the establishment, control and funding of mechanics' institutes. Expanded population throughout the 1800s led to an increase in a variety of libraries, including subscription and free public libraries. Much of the population was served by libraries under the direction of local school authorities. In the late 1860s and 1870s, as the Dominion of Canada began to take shape, small amounts of centralized financial support for libraries became available.

In 1882 Ontario passed a Free Libraries act, and this was soon followed in 1891 by one in British Columbia. Carnegie's influence was felt in Canada as elsewhere. Approximately 125 Carnegie supported libraries were built in the early 1900s. Funding for regional library programs also was included. In 1933, the publication of *Libraries in Canada* resulted from a major study by a commission of "ministers of the federal government, premiers and ministers in each of the provinces, officials of education departments, principals of normal schools, librarians in all sorts and sizes of libraries, newspaper editors, businessmen, leaders of labour and farmers movements" (Encyclopedia of Library and Information Science, 1976).

The Canadian Library Association was founded in 1946. In 1949 as a result of the establishment of a National Bibliographic Centre, selected national services became available. Today's Canadian libraries are under the jurisdiction of the provinces, not of the federal government. "The provincial legislation specifies the method of establishment, the services to be provided and the means of support" (Canada Yearbook, 1978:316). In the late 1940s regional library service was developed to meet more efficiently the needs of small towns and rural areas. Regional services are widely used by most Canadian provinces. Parliament established the National Library of Canada in 1953. There is federal financial support of the National Library as well as of the public systems of the Northwest Territories and the Yukon.

> The Federal Government of Canada is responsible for the financial support of The Library of Parliament, the National Library, the National Science Library, the libraries of the government departments, the Royal Commissions, the crown Corporations, the Public Library Service of the Northwest Territories, the Yukon Regional Library system, and the development of library service to the 558 Indian bands. (Encyclopedia of Library and Information Science, 1976:73)

The services of the libraries vary greatly from province to province, just as the provinces themselves differ ethnically and historically. In fact, many government publications are bilingual.

> Canada's philosophy of nationhood imposes on libraries the responsibility of preserving, promoting, and distributing by print, manuscript, and mass media the heritage of the nations who are now part of the Canadian people. This task, primarily a provincial one, is also a responsibility of the Federal Government, of Canada's National Library, National Film Board and National Gallery, and the Canadian Broadcasting Commission. (Encyclopedia of Library and Information Science 1976:75)

United States

According to Johnson and Harris (1976) "Small private libraries existed from the very first in the Pilgrim and Puritan colonies in Massachusetts." Some of the notable libraries of the 17th century included Cotton Mather's in Massachusetts, Robert Hunt's in Virginia and James Logan's in Philadelphia. These collections typically reflected the owner's need for information of a specialized sort.

Probably the first attempt at a public library in the colonies came in 1656 when Captain Robert Keayne, a merchant of

Boston willed his book collection to the town for a public library, stipulating that the town build a suitable building to house it. (Johnson and Harris, 1976:198)

While the collection did not grow, the building did serve as a repository for town records for nearly a hundred years. A fire totally destroyed the building in 1747.

Social libraries came into existence in the 18th century. This involved a process of pooling privately owned books for study, debating and social activities. A significant development occurred in 1731 when Benjamin Franklin worked to establish the first subscription library in Philadelphia. This was soon followed by commercial or circulating libraries that made material available on a fee basis. Other libraries, including mercantile and mechanics', preceeded the development of the public library.

In 1789 some states established libraries for government use. "By 1876 every state and territory had a government library whose purpose was:

1. To collect and preserve complete sets of all publications of the state or territory, as far as possible.
2. To collect works in American History, especially of the states or territories" (Gates, 1968:77).

In 1833 Peterborough, New Hampshire, established what has become recognized as the first modern public library in the United States and by 1850 the need for public libraries was becoming more widely acknowledged. For example, the report of the trustees of the Boston Public Library indicated:

Reading ought to be furnished to all, as a matter of public policy and duty, on the same principle that we furnish free education. . . . We, as a people, are constantly required to decide, either ignorantly or wisely. (Cited in: Johnson and Harris, 1976)

From this it can be understood that the "informed citizen" would be the future of a democratic country. The Boston Public Library was opened in 1854. Three important developments occurred at the end of the 1880s. The American Library association was formed in 1876. A report on public libraries in the United States was issued that established systematic standards for public libraries. Finally, Andrew Carnegie, the great benefactor of libraries, began giving money to towns to provide library buildings. Between 1886 and 1919 he supported the building of 2,509 libraries and had spent over $50,000,000 in the English speaking world. Nearly 1500 libraries were built in the United States and hundreds more in Canada and Great Britain.

By the late 1800s the states were beginning to grant monies directly to libraries. In 1890 Massachusetts formed the first state library commission. County library systems also appeared in areas where county government was strong. Libraries continued their growth in the U.S., a development slowed only by the Great Depression. At that time, expenditures for libraries were limited even while use was increasing. Several major reports appeared in the 1940s and 1950s that set the direction for the modern public library.

In 1956 Congress passed the Library Services Act, which provided federal aid to libraries in rural areas. The state extension unit administered these funds. Eight years later the Library Services and Construction Act extended funds, on a matching basis, to urban as well as rural areas for building and renovation.

The American Library Association published "Minimum Standards for Public Library Systems, 1966." This document provided not only standards, but clarified the goals of public libraries as well. These standards were designed to provide for equalized services throughout various library systems. The report encouraged the use of cooperatives and library systems, thus facilitating the sharing of assets.

The National Commission on Libraries and Information Science issued a final report in 1975, which specified national objectives including:

a. basic minimums of library and information services
b. special services to special constituencies,
c. continuing education for personnel,
d. including the private sector in development.

Earlier we described modern libraries in Great Britain as functioning with the British Library as the hub of its system. Public libraries in the United States are best described as being state directed, with the Library of Congress serving mainly as a resource for special needs and programs. As an example, the Library of Congress provides services for the handicapped that are not made available by the states. Each state has its own statues that establish the conditions for library services and specify how taxes and public funds can be used. The arrangement, of course, varies from state to state. Each state has a government library as well as a state library extension agency. The latter serves to extend library services throughout the state in areas not adequately covered by local systems. In some states county or regional systems also serve these functions.

What do these systems have in common from the viewpoint of a criminologist? For one thing, regardless of how they were developed, the primary goal of public service interacts with some of the factors related to crime. Secondly, there is no "typical" library in these systems. Rather, there is a wide range of institutions and potential problems. Further, as public institutions these libraries are affected by both the good and bad happenings within the local community.

RISK FACTORS

Are there features of the library, the public library in particular, that are likely to facilitate crime and disruption? Unfortunately, there are a number of these risk factors. While many of the factors affect public institutions in general and not just libraries, some are more common in the library setting. At times the risk of crime is increased by conditions that are beyond the control of the library, while other problems can be reduced by library policies. At this point we will summarize the major risk factors, but leave the description of major crime reduction techniques for the final chapter. The intervening chapters present data from studies that examine the relationship between crime and many of these risk factors.

Ease of access. There are a number of risk factors that facilitate the likelihood of crime and disruption in libraries. Chief among these for public libraries and many academic libraries is the ease of access. Many of the problems of theft and most of the problems caused by problem patrons are exacerbated by the ease of access. Most thefts are crimes of opportunity. During the first national study of crime in U.S. libraries (Lincoln, 1984), one theme expressed over and over again was the problem generated by open access. One library director sent us a copy of a sign that summarized the problem well: "This is a public library—protect your property!" Academic and special libraries have varying degrees of visitor and patron controls that help limit some of the problems typically found in public libraries. However, ease of access is not the only problem that must be considered.

Desirable contents. Most public libraries contain many desirable and easily sold goods including books, AV equipment and materials, artwork, cash, antiques and so on. The availability of these items is an attraction to the potential thief. Chapter 6 presents a variety of strategies for protecting these items from damage and theft. Thus, despite the availability of targeted items, the risk can be reduced.

Age of patrons. Data to be presented later shows that the young tend to be disproportionately involved with crime. This is a good example of a factor that tends to be beyond the control of libraries. Assuming that access by the young will not be curtailed, libraries that serve large numbers of juveniles should recognize the potential risks presented by this group and adopt appropriate security measures.

The schedule. The operating hours of many public libraries also facilitate certain kinds of crime and disruption. It is not uncommon to find that the public library is the only public building open at night or on weekends. The extended hours coupled with the ease of access make the library a particularly attractive setting for "street people" and potential offenders.

Lack of security. It has been suggested (Lincoln and Lincoln, 1980) that compared with other public buildings such as schools, museums, arenas, etc., libraries are relatively unsecured. For example, a comparison of Massachusetts school and public libraries found that a significantly higher proportion of schools had operational security systems and programs. This relative lack of security may itself be a risk factor. Given the fact that libraries have open access and valued goods, security policies and programs should be in place. As schools and other public areas continue to become more secure settings, much of the crime directed at schools may be displaced to the less secure but equally inviting library.

Crime prevention training. Along with the relative lack of security many staff members tend to be untrained in security techniques. Library professionals increasingly are becoming aware of the need for training in personal and property crime prevention, yet most have not become involved in any type of training programs. While there are no guarantees that training will improve safety, most professionals who work with the public can benefit from increased awareness of crime prevention skills.

Building design. An additional factor related to security risks is the design of library buildings. Admittedly, newer construction and renovation often takes security issues into account. Vision enhancement is one example of the relationship between building design and security. But most older library facilities were built before there was a perceived need to secure the building or the entire collection. Many of these buildings have too many exits and entrances and hidden areas that are difficult to monitor.

Activity level. The level of activity within many libraries may facilitate crime. In many cases there is not time for the staff to attend to potential problem patrons or to keep an eye on every potential book thief. These problems are intensified in the smaller one- and two-person libraries. There are so many professional activities that must be accomplished in the typical public library that staff members cannot devote extensive time to security issues. Multiple demands on the staff often require them to move from place to place within the facility, occasionally on a predictable schedule. Potential thieves, anticipating this schedule, simply may wait for the target area to be unsupervised. At times there are so many patrons using the library that it is impossible to oversee even a small proportion of them. Even if it were possible, it is not clear that this is an appropriate responsibility for the professional librarian.

Legislation. In an attempt to reduce crime, librarians often lobby for "improved legislation." The existence of laws designed to protect the library and facilitate prosecution of offenders can be a deterrent to crime. However, legislation is not always successful in preventing crime in the library. For example, much of the early legislation in the United States was ambiguous, not clearly specifying what was a crime. These early laws typically dealt with detention of materials and provided minimal sanctions for violators. Furthermore, according to Peter Parker (1984:78), it is not clear wether special library crime legislation is needed. "Most criminal codes protect property owners against theft, malicious mischief and vandalism. Consequently, it is more important for administrators to identify those particular parts of library operations that are not covered by existing laws and to remedy those deficiencies than it is for them to work for the passage of a more general library law that supposedly covers all contingencies" (p. 78). The more recent legislation has focused on the theft of materials from libraries and often has harsher penalties.

The effective use of existing or modified legislation depends upon the successful resolution of several potential problems. Often the first problem involves the staff. They first must be aware of the provisions of the legislation and then be willing to make contact with a violator when necessary. There may be certain risks involved in confronting an offender. These risks may have to do with either personal safety or personal liability. Staff training can provide appropriate guidelines for how and when to (or when not to) confront and detain an offender. It should be recognized that attempts to detain a suspect may lead to the use of a level of force that is undesirable from a safety standpoint. Futhermore, not all legislation protects the librarian from liability when confronting an offender. However, the most recent legislation passed in several American states does protect the staff member acting with a reasonable belief that a crime is being committed.

Once problems related to staff response are resolved, it is still necessary to have cooperation from those in the criminal justice system. For example, local police must be willing to respond when necessary. If they are to do this, they will have to perceive that the problems are real and serious. If the attitude of local police is that the problems in the library are of low priority because "there are REAL crimes out there," then they should be brought up to date on the frequency, cost, and potential danger of the episodes occurring in the library. Police cooperation is an essential first step in using the criminal justice system. Secondly, the police have to be able to respond quickly to a call from the library. It is an unreasonable burden for a librarian to detain a suspect for more than a brief time. Finally, the police must be willing to carry out an investigation when necessary. That is, they must devote the time and effort necessary to properly prepare and follow a case to its conclusion.

Even if effective legislation is in place, the staff are well trained and cooperative, and the local police are supportive, legislation will be ineffective without appropriate policies about prosecution. There must be a willingness to prosecute cases both by the library administration and the local prosecutors. Since not all cases will be selected for prosecution, there should be recognized guidelines indicating when prosecution is warranted. A consistent failure to prosecute will weaken the effect of the legislation and might even lead to an increase in library crime. Crime against the library is likely to escalate if it becomes apparent to those contemplating crime that the administration is "all talk and no action."

Attitudes of the public. Crime also is likely to occur when there is both opportunity and a social climate that offers support for the illegal activity. The opportunity within the library has been demonstrated. The social support rests on personal beliefs. If there are substantial numbers of people in the community who believe that the unauthorized taking or keeping of library materials is not a crime, then the problems may be difficult to control. It is not uncommon for people to have more tolerant attitudes about the treatment of public resources than for comparable private resources. Patrons who never return books don't think of themselves as "stealing." They often seem to have a "first come, first served" attitude about library materials. This tolerance of deviant behavior may be coupled with the belief that the library is a "safe target." Potential offenders may believe that the library provides the opportunity for successful crime and, as mentioned above, that the staff is not likely to take any legal action.

Attitudes of librarians. Tolerance of questionable behavior often extends to the professional staff as well. Although we have seen evidence of change, many librarians tend to ignore actions that managers and administrators of other facilities would not tolerate. For example, books may be considered "long overdue" rather than stolen. At some point it should become evident that there is no intention to return the material and that it is being treated as the patron's own property. Many items are labeled lost when they don't appear in an inventory. It is likely that a sizable proportion of those items are in effect stolen. It is essential to set reasonable standards for what is appropriate behavior for both staff and patron within the library setting. The public cannot be expected to set harsher standards than those demonstrated by the staff.

Given this wide variety of risk factors, it is important to view the public library and its problems within the context of the community setting. Crime in the library should not be viewed in isolation. What happens in the library is influenced not only by the characteristics of the library itself but also by the characteristics of the community in which the library is located. Behavior that is common in the neighborhood around the library may spill over from the street to the library. If, for example, the neighborhood is plagued by vandals, then the library in that area is more likely to experience vandalism. A community experiencing racial or ethnic conflict may have libraries that reflect these same antagonisms between patrons or against the staff.

In the chapters that follow we present the findings from three national studies of library crime and disruption. The first to be presented is the study of England, Scotland, and Wales. Chapter 3 provides information on a major study of Canadian libraries. Comparisons between problems in the United States, Canada, and Great Britain appear in Chapter 4. Comparative library security patterns are emphasized in Chapter 5. An extensive checklist of security options concludes the volume.

REFERENCES

Camp, John F., "Security systems," in American Library Association Yearbook, (Chicago: ALA, 1985), pp. 258-259.
Canada Yearbook, Ministry of Industry, Trade and Commerce, (Quebec: 1978).
Encyclopedia of Library and Information Science, (New York: Marcel Dekker, Inc., 1976).
Gates, Jean K. *Introduction to Librarianship*, (New York: McGraw Hill, 1968).
Hookway, T. T., "The British library," in W. L. Saunders, (Ed.) *British Librarianship Today*, (London: The Library Association, 1976) pp. 37-45.
Johnson, Elmer D., and Harris, Michael H., *History of Libraries in the Western World*, (Metuchen, New Jersey: The Scarecrow Press, Inc., 1976).
Lincoln, Alan J., *Crime in the Library: A Study of Patterns, Impact and Security*, (New York: R. R. Bowker, 1984).
Lincoln, Alan J. and Lincoln, Carol Z., "The impact of crime in public libraries," *Library and Archival Security*, 3, (1980):125-137.
Parker, Peter, "Statutory protection of library materials," *Library Trends*, 33, (1984):77-94.
Phillips, B. J., "Public libraries: Legislation, administration and finance," (London: The Library Association, 1977).
Predeek, Albert, *A History of Libraries in Great Britain and North America*, (Chicago: ALA, 1947).
Stewart, Linda, "Never mind the answer, what's the question?," (Loughborough, England: Centre for Library and Information Management, 1984).
Wilson, Alexander, "Public libraries," in W. L. Saunders (Ed.) *British Librarianship Today*, (London: The Library Association, 1976) pp. 170-203.

Chapter Two

Library Crime in Great Britain

We have seen that crime and disruption in public buildings, including libraries, often reflects the patterns of crime in the surrounding community. An urban library tends to have crime and disruption problems similar to those of other urban libraries but distinct from problems in the smaller libraries. Libraries in rural areas may have much in common with each other when it comes to problems of crime, but are unlike their urban counterparts. Similar patterns may be found even when comparing problems across national borders. That is, a large British library may have more in common with a large American or Canadian library than with a small British institution.

There are several reasons for these cross-cultural similarities. Admittedly, there are differences in the general patterns of crime between countries. Yet within these general differences there may be corresponding similarities between factors influencing crime and crime patterns. For example, even though the general crime patterns of England, Scotland, Wales, Canada and the United States differ from one another (some more than others), the relationships between age and the likelihood of committing an offense can be quite similar.

It is important to understand the general crime pattern in a country before trying to interpret the significance of library crime and disruption. We will begin with a brief overview of British crime patterns and then turn to the study of crime and disruption in Great Britain's public libraries. The costs of crime will then be examined. The emphasis here, corresponding to the focus of the library crime study itself, will be on crime patterns in England, Wales, and Scotland.

In 1982 there were slightly less than four million notifiable offenses in England, Wales, and Scotland. As can be seen in Table 2.1 the majority of these were crimes of theft and handling of stolen goods. Since both the legal systems and the mechanisms for report-

Table 2.1
Crimes in Great Britain

Crime	England and Wales (1982)	Scotland (1981)
Personal violence	108,700	8,000
Sexual offenses	19,700	4,800
Burglary	810,600	95,700
Robbery	22,800	4,200
Theft/stolen goods	1,755,900	200,800
Fraud/forgery	123,100	21,400
Criminal damage	417,800	61,700
Other offenses	3,800	11,300
TOTAL OFFENSES	3,262,400	407,900

Data adapted from Home Office reports.

ing and counting crimes differ somewhat, the figures for Scottish crimes have been adjusted so that they are consistent with those reported for England and Wales.

As is typical of most industrialized nations, the most serious crimes occur least often. For example, while there were nearly two million theft related offenses in the three nations, there were fewer than 120,000 crimes of violence and fewer than 25,000 sexual offenses. However, the relative probability of occurrence is not a good indicator of the level of concern about crime. Numerous studies have shown that the public tends to worry most about these serious crimes. To illustrate, although violent crimes account for less than 3% and sexual offenses for less than 1% of total crimes, concern is greatest about these crimes that are least likely to occur.

There is a problem with using the reported or officially recorded crime statistics such as those shown in Table 2.1. In many instances these may be underestimates of the actual number of crimes. Many crimes go undetected or unreported. Others may be reported but not officially recorded. The actual rate of reporting varies with the type of crime. While burglary involving highly valued items is quite likely to be reported to police, minor thefts and sexual offenses are far less likely to be reported. The thefts may go unreported because the minor losses are not considered sufficiently disruptive to justify the cost of involvement with the criminal justice system. In contrast, sexual offenses often go unreported because the experienced effects are already so disruptive that additional involvement is seen as unmanageable by the victim.

CRIME TRENDS

Crime in Great Britain has shown a general pattern of increase. The incidence of both violent and property crime has been increasing significantly over the last 25 years. The more rapid increase has been in crimes of violence. In 1961, there were approximately 18,000 known violent crimes in England and Wales. By 1971 the number had increased to 47,000; and by 1982 there were 109,000 known crimes of violence against the person. The increase in crime has been much greater than the increase in population during the comparable period. Since 1961 the rate of violent crime has increased about 500 per cent. For every 100,000 people in 1961, there were about 39 violent crimes, while in 1971 the rate had grown to 96 per 100,000. By 1980 the violent crime rate was approximately 200.

The increase in property crime for the same period was not as dramatic. There were, as indicated, many more property crimes than violent crimes, but the rate of increase was lower. For example, in 1961 there were about 750,000 property crimes in England and Wales, a rate of 1,625. By 1979 there were over two million such offenses, a rate of about 4,250. Slightly different patterns were evident in Scotland. Between 1971 and 1981 violent offenses increased 60% while property offenses increased approximately 70%.

Although Canada, Great Britain and the United States have been experiencing increases in the crime rate, significant differences exist between the nations. Perhaps the most striking difference is in the homicide rates. For every 100,000 people there were 1.2 homicides in England and Wales in 1979. In contrast, Canada had a rate of 2.7, while the United States rate was 9.7. Not only are there differences in the rates of homicide but in the method of murder as well. Only 9% of Britain's homicides involve guns, and a small proportion of these are handguns. In the United States about half of all murders involve the use of handguns. The impact of both legislation (affecting the availability of guns) and cultural values (importance of guns) can be seen here.

Characteristics of Offenders

What is known about the identity of potential or actual offenders? There is one outstanding feature that tends to hold true in most places. The young are disproportionately represented in the perpetration of crime. While the very young tend to commit few crimes, adolescents and young adults are the high-risk age groups. In 1981 over half of all males found guilty of indictable offenses were under the age of 21. Table 2.2 contains more detailed information on the

Table 2.2

Offenders Found Guilty by Age, 1981

Crime	Age (% of total)			
	10-13	14-16	17-20	+20
Murder	--	04	20	76
Other personal violence	03	15	30	52
Sex offenses	04	16	19	60
Burglary	13	29	28	30
Robbery	05	19	34	41
Theft	13	23	23	41
Fraud/forgery	01	05	20	74
Criminal damage	15	21	30	34
TOTAL CRIMES	10	20	25	45
Total Rate/1,000	30	75	73	13

Data adapted from Home Office Reports.

relationship between involvement in crime and the age of the known offender. Notice that the likelihood of the crime being committed by a young person (under 21) varies with the specific crime. While less than a fourth of crimes involving a death were committed by the young, over two-thirds of burglaries involved this age group. Overall, the rate of being guilty of or cautioned for indictable offenses peaked at 14-16 (75 per 1,000), remained relatively stable for 17- to 20-year-olds (73 per 1,000) and dropped significantly for those over 21 (13 per 1,000). The decline after the age of 21 occurs quite rapidly.

The importance of age also is apparent when examining the arrest data for females. It is important to note, however, that females are involved in the criminal justice system far less often than are males. When they are, however, the effect of their age is similar to that for males. The peak risk age of offense is between 14-16. It is probable that these general trends and patterns of crime in Great Britain are reflected in crimes affecting the library.

PROCEDURE

The survey research on crime and disruption in Great Britain's libraries was conducted in July and August of 1984. The survey is a revision of an instrument first used in a similar project for U.S. public libraries. It included 65 items focusing on the characteristics of the library and the community, 24 types of crime and disruption, the costs of crime and the use of 14 different security items or programs. The research sample of 300 libraries included the central library in each district in England, Wales and Scotland. In addition, a systematic sample of every third regional library in each district was included. This sample clearly is not representative of all libraries, but rather of the larger libraries in each district.

The research was conducted with the suppport of the Centre for Library and Information Management (CLAIM) at the University of Loughborough. The cover letter included with each survey mentioned this sponsorship and the fact that the study was a follow-up to a previous study done in the United States. Respondents were assured of the anonymity of each responding library and asked to return the survey to CLAIM in the preaddressed, enclosed envelope.

Characteristics of Sampled Libraries

Three hundred libraries were sampled using the procedure described above. At the time of analysis, 209 usable surveys had been returned. Unlike what occurred in the Canadian and U.S. studies, this procedure resulted in a sample that is not completely representative of British public libraries. Thus, it is important to describe the characteristics of the libraries included in the analysis so that appropriate comparisons can be made.

City Size

The sample included libraries from all sizes of cities and towns. However, one third of the returns were from libraries in cities between 100,000 and 500,000. Another 28% came from cities of 10,000 to 50,000. Approximately 10% each came from towns under 10,000 and cities over 500,000. The complete breakdown of the sample is shown in Table 2.3. The relationship between city size and the level of crime in the library will be discussed later in this chapter.

Institutional Factors

Number of patrons. One measure of the activity level of the institution is the number of patrons that use the facility on an average day. The range of possible responses to this question was from "1-10" to "over 1,000." None of the respondents indicated that they served less than 30 patrons per day. As evident in Table 2.4 the most common response was between "250 and 500 patrons daily." More than 90% of the institutions served more than 100 patrons each day. Twenty-two percent estimated that there were over 1,000 patrons on a typical day.

Annual circulation. A second indicator of the activity level of the library is the annual circulation. Here we find a wide variation in activity—from 3,000 items reported by one library, to over 1,000,000 reported by nearly a quarter (23.9%) of the sample. The summary of annual circulation of the sampled libraries is shown in Table 2.4.

Staff size. Previous studies (Lincoln, 1984) have shown that crime patterns are related to both the activity level and the size of the library. Staff size is a good indicator of both of these factors.

Table 2.3

City Size of Sampled Libraries

City size	%	Number
<2,500	01	n=2
2.5-10,000	11	n=21
10-50,000	28	n=56
50-100,000	16	n=32
100-500,000	35	n=69
>500,000	10	n=19
Missing response		n=10
Total		n=209

Table 2.4

Characteristics of Sampled Libraries

# Patrons/Day	%	Annual Circulation	%
<30	00	<25,000	08
31-50	02	25-50,000	02
51-100	07	51-99,000	06
101-250	23	100-499,000	46
251-500	25	>500,000	38
501-1,000	20		
>1,000	22		

Staff size was measured in four separate categories: (1) professional staff, (2) aides/assistants, (3) security personnel and (4) other staff (usually custodial). Professional staff ranged from 21% of the sample with one professional librarian to 5% reporting over 50 professional staff members. Half of the sample had fewer than four fulltime professionals. (See Table 2.5.) The average number of professional librarians was just under 11.

The use of aides/assistants, as expected, was common. All respondents employed at least one assistant, while half had nine or more nonprofessional staff members. In contrast, security personnel

Table 2.5
Proportion of Libraries with Various Number of Employees

Number	Librarians	Aides	Security	Total
0	3%	<1	68	0
1	21	5	12	1
2-5	40	29	14	19
6-10	14	26	2	13
11-25	10	23	2	32
26-50	7	7	2	21
+50	5	11	1	14

were relatively rare. Two-thirds of those reporting had no security personnel. Less than 10% had more than three security employees. An employee index was computed as an indicator of the activity level of the library. As shown in the "total" category of Table 2.5, 15% had fewer than five employees and 13% had between 6 and 10 staff members. Large staffs (over 50 employees) were found in 14% of the sample.

PATTERNS OF CRIME

There are many ways to categorize the variety of crimes that occur in a community. Basic distinctions often are made between crimes against people and crimes against property. An alternative simple classification scheme might consider violent and nonviolent crimes. The United States Department of Justice differentiates between serious and other offenses (Type I and Type II offenses). In this scheme, data are recorded for eight serious and about 30 other offenses. The Scottish Home and Health Department organizes crime reporting into seven groups including nonsexual crimes of violence, crimes involving indecency, crimes involving dishonesty, and so on. The British Home Office reports describe crimes of violence against the person, sexual offenses, burglary, criminal damage, and so on. When comparing crime patterns across cultures, it is necessary to maintain a degree of flexibility because of the variation in categorizing crime.

In our library crime research projects we were not as concerned with actual legal categories as we were with behavioral categories that described the type of offense. For example, we asked about several different kinds of vandalism that were likely to cause problems in maintaining a secure library. Intentional damage to books, equipment, the building, etc. were examined. In most legal systems these would be collapsed into one type of crime (i.e., criminal damage or malicious and reckless conduct.) Our concern has been to maximize the information available to library administrators and staff regardless of national classification categories and legal codes.

The study of Great Britain's public libraries examined 24 separate types of crime and disruption. Not all of these would meet the legal definition of a crime. For example, minor verbal abuse of a librarian might not meet the criteria of a crime established by existing statutes. Some other offenses might not be *socially perceived* as a crime, even though they do meet the legal criteria. In this category we might find book damage, minor drug use, and even the unauthorized taking of a book. It is not uncommon for social and legal definitions of crime to be at odds. Similarly, there may be regional differences as well. In one location deliberately detaining a book may be a crime, while in others it is not. Local ordinances vary with regard to what is permissible in public buildings such as libraries. These differences are compounded when conducting national or cross national studies.

The 24 categories of crime and disruption have been combined into the more general categories of theft, vandalism/destruction, problem patron behavior and assault. The complete listing is shown in Table 2.6. A critical question in survey research of this type is "How accurate are the reports of crime likely to be?" Several general concerns about victimization surveys should be mentioned. The surveys asked respondents to tell us about some behavior that the perpetrator would be trying to hide. For example, drug sales in the library are likely to be carried out in isolated areas such as bathrooms and behind the stacks. It is unlikely that our respondents knew about all of these and other hidden offenses. There are several other reasons that these estimates of crime may be low. Even when a crime was known to someone in the library, our respondent may

Table 2.6

Percentage of Libraries Reporting Crime and Disruption

Type of Episode	\multicolumn{6}{c}{Number of Episodes}					
	0	1-2	3-5	6-10	11-20	20+
Book damage	13	18	18	18	9	25
Vandalism outside	24	29	16	14	5	11
Vandalism inside	48	21	13	8	5	5
Equipment damage	77	15	3	3	2	1
Damage staff car	83	14	3	1	0	0
Damage patron car	90	7	1	1	1	1
Arson	86	12	2	0	0	0
Book theft	9	7	9	10	10	55
Reference theft	24	19	17	14	12	14
A V theft	67	9	8	4	4	8
Equipment theft	59	30	6	1	1	4
Fraudulent bill	92	5	3	1	1	0
Counterfeit money	91	4	4	0	1	1
Personal theft	43	44	8	3	2	1
Other theft	44	34	11	3	2	6
Forced entry	58	27	10	4	1	1
Drug use	88	7	2	1	1	1
Drug sales	98	0	0	2	1	0
Harassed patron	48	25	11	7	4	5
Harassed staff	26	21	21	11	10	13
Obscene calls	73	16	6	2	2	2
Indecent exposure	87	9	2	2	1	0
Assault on patron	92	6	1	1	1	0
Assault on staff	85	14	1	0	1	0
INDICES:						
Vandalism	4	8	12	16	20	40
Theft	4	1	7	11	15	63
Problem Patron	16	18	17	19	9	22
Assault	83	13	3	0	1	1
Total	1	2	4	2	10	81

have not been informed and thus could not relay the information to us. Many episodes may have been known but not reported because it was felt to be "none of our business," "a breach of security," "a perceived sign of poor administration" and so on. Overall, we suspect that these specific studies and other victimization studies of public institutions tend to underestimate the actual level of crime and disruption.

Data from the research project can be reported in several different ways. The first approach involves using the library as the focus of analysis. In this approach the research questions might include: How many libraries experience the crimes? What percentage of libraries have no crime, low levels of crime, high crime, etc.? What factors relate to being a high crime or a low crime library? A second approach would involve focusing on the crimes. We then could ask: How often do the crimes occur? What is the average number of each type of crime? What is the rate of theft, vandalism, assault, etc.? Both approaches provide useful descriptive information and, in our view, should be used together.

Vandalism/Destruction

Most public facilities experience some vandalism. At times the level is low and the vandalism is nothing more than a nuisance. At other times there is so much damage that the institution cannot function adequately. We examined 7 different problems of vandalism and destruction ranging from intentional book damage to damage to patrons' cars to arson. What such incidents have in common is the intent to damage public or private property. Furthermore, vandalism results in destruction that usually is visible to the public. It serves as a constant reminder that there is a problem with crime and disruption. The level of vandalism in a particular library may be far less than the level of theft, but the public is more likely to see the results of the vandalism. Vandals may be influenced by different motives, including the desire to further a cause, to gain revenge, to express anger aimed at symbolic targets or to impress one's friends. Vandalism is, therefore, an important but difficult problem to manage.

> Petty, mindless vandalism is always a problem. This usually comes from 14-18 year olds. The behavior just seems so pointless.

Intentional book damage. Mutilation of books in the library was one of the most common crimes reported. Over 85% of the reports indicated at least one known episode of intentional book damage. Several others indicated that there was damage to books but that whether or not it was intentional was not known for certain. Eighteen percent of the libraries reported only one or two episodes, while an additional 18% had 3-5 occurrences. One fourth of the sample had over 20 cases of book mutilation during the year. (See Table 2.6.) It should be pointed out that the survey was worded in a way that asked about the number of times that each problem occurred. This is not the same as the number of books that were damaged. One episode of mutilation may have involved multiple volumes. The same reasoning would apply for episodes of book theft and so on. In previous studies (Lincoln, 1984; Lincoln and Lincoln, 1980) the definition of chronic problems was set at six or more episodes of the same crime in one year. Using that same criterion, exactly half of the institutions were experiencing chronic intentional book damage. The average frequency of intentional book damage was 9.8. This is equivalent to a rate of 980 episodes per 100 libraries. Crime rates are presented in Table 2.7.

Vandalism outside the building. Perhaps the most visible offense against a public library would be acts of vandalism that defaced or damaged the exterior of the building. In these cases both patrons and nonpatrons would be aware of the problem. Decisions about using or not using the facility might be influenced by the visible damage to the buildings or grounds. Three quarters of the reports indicated at least one case of vandalism outside the building. Approximately 30% knew of one or two episodes, while 16% reported 3-5 cases. At the other extreme, 11% reported over 20 cases of this type of vandalism during the year. Thirty-one percent had chronic vandalism outside the facility (6 or more cases). The rate of vandalism outside the building was 574 (per 100 libraries).

> Vandalism is commonplace but tends to be concentrated in certain areas—broken windows, damage to trees and external fixtures, etc. Nearly always happens when the library is closed.

Vandalism inside the building. Cases of intentional damage to the inside of the library were less frequent than those to the outside of the building. This is to be expected, given the vulnerability of the outside of buildings. Just over half of our sample (52%) experienced some vandalism inside the library. Twenty-one percent reported one or two cases, and 13% told us of 3-5 repetitions. Only 5% had more than 20 cases during the year. On average, each library had 3.5 cases per year.

Table 2.7

Crime Rates for British Libraries

Type of Episode	Rate per 100 Libraries
Book damage	986
Vandalism outside	575
Vandalism inside	348
Equipment damage	101
Damage staff car	31
Damage patron car	43
Arson	21
Book theft	1,656
Reference theft	739
A V theft	340
Equipment theft	166
Fraudulent bill	33
Counterfeit money	60
Personal theft	156
Other theft	293
Forced entry	136
Drug use	80
Drug sales	20
Harassed patron	329
Harassed staff	672
Obscene calls	132
Indecent exposure	41
Assault on patron	23
Assault on staff	27
INDICES:	
Vandalism	2,072
Theft	3,498
Problem Patron	1,235
Assault	49
Total	6,922

We spend quite a bit of time and money repairing vandalized furniture and windows.

Vandalism to equipment. There are many valuable pieces of equipment in most public libraries. This is certainly true of the libraries sampled in Great Britain. Photocopying equipment, audiovisual equipment, storage items, computer equipment and convenience equipment such as coin changers and vending machines all may become targets for vandals. Damage to equipment was not as common as book damage or building damage. However, nearly one quarter of the responses noted at least one episode of equipment being vandalized. In 15% of the libraries there were one or two cases while 5% reported six or more separate incidents. The rate of vandalism to equipment was 101.

Vandalism of staff/patron's cars. Parking areas around public buildings often are favored targets of vandals and thieves. Two survey questions assessed the incidence of damage to cars owned by library staff and by library patrons. Library staff were more likely to report their cars being damaged by vandals. Nearly one-fifth of these responses included an instance of cars being damaged intentionally. The vast majority of these reports were of one or two episodes, with only 3% of the respondents noting more than two cases. Cars belonging to patrons were reportedly damaged in only 10% of the returned surveys. Undoubtedly many other cases occurred but were not made known to library staff. Only 4% of respondents mentioned more than two cases.

Arson. There are few crimes that have the potential of producing greater damage than does arson. It is true that much arson results in property damage only, but the potential for serious personal injury or death is always present. One out of seven libraries indicated that they had experienced a case of arson. Nearly all of these libraries reported only one such episode. Two or more repetitions were experienced by 3% of the sample. For every 100 libraries there were 21 reported cases of arson.

> Vandalism was a serious problem a year ago—library was actually burned down by vandals. However, situation has improved dramatically after attempts to involve teenagers in library activity.

Vandalism index. An index which included all of the vandalism/destruction items was computed as an overall measure of the amount of damage to the library. The overwhelming majority of libraries had some vandalism during the year. Only 3% reportedly were free of intentional acts of vandalism. Twenty-five percent had 5 or fewer repetitions, and an additional quarter of the sample reported between 6 and 15 cases. One fourth of the reports indicated that there were 30 or more known offenses involving vandalism. The average number of cases of vandalism was 21 per year. That is a rate of 2100 episodes of vandalism for every 100 public libraries.

Theft

The crime patterns described earlier in this chapter clearly showed that theft by far was the most common crime in England, Wales and Scotland. Overall, the same pattern holds for libraries in this sample. We asked about 8 specific kinds of theft as well as incidents of breaking and entering, which often precede an actual theft. These ranged from the obvious problem of book theft to theft of AV materials and equipment and the passing of counterfeit money. Once again it is likely that only some of the thefts that occurred were known and reported to us. Generally, the more serious or costly the theft, the greater the likelihood that it will be discovered and reported. For example, studies conducted by the United States Department of Justice indicate that less than 30% of thefts of less than $100.00 are reported to authorities, while over 60% of thefts of $250.00 are reported (U.S. Department of Justice, 1983).

Books. Over 90% of the libraries we surveyed included at least one episode of book theft. In fact, book theft was a crime that occurred with some regularity. While 7% of the respondents had 1 or 2 cases, 55% reported over 20 episodes of book theft. When over 20 cases were reported, this was computed as 25 incidents thus keeping the estimated rate of book theft low. A better estimate of total book losses is provided later. Our measure of chronic book theft (over six episodes) included exactly three fourths of the libraries. An episode is not the same as a single volume being stolen. Many of the so-called episodes involved the theft of dozens of separate volumes. Since book theft was anticipated to be the most common offense in the libraries, an additional question asked respondents to estimate the number of volumes (books and journals) stolen during the year. This is not an easy question to answer. Unless there is some type of regular complete or partial inventory or an ongoing computerized circulation system, missing books are not likely to be noticed. It is not surprising that nearly 40% of respondents did not answer this question. Of those that did provide an estimate of stolen volumes, one third reported 15 or fewer volumes stolen, one third reported between 15 and 200 stolen volumes and one third knew of between 200 and 1,000 volumes being stolen. Over 10% of the sample indicated that more than 1,000 volumes were known to be stolen during the year. Conservatively, the average book loss due to theft was just over 250 volumes per year. The figure is conservative because losses of over 1,000 volumes were recorded as 999 lost volumes, thus keeping the average deflated. If these figures are converted to rates, then over 25,000 volumes were stolen from each 100 libraries.

> We have a problem keeping popular material in sufficient quantities to reduce theft.

> Much sensitive and valuable material has to be kept in reserve stock because it tends to be stolen.

> The loss of stock by default, failing to return legitimately borrowed books, is a serious problem amounting in 1983/1984 to over 3,000 volumes.

Reference material. Although not as common as book theft, the theft of reference material was a chronic problem in many libraries. Nearly one quarter indicated that they knew of no problems of reference theft. Nineteen percent had only one or two cases, while 17% reported 3-5 thefts. Forty percent of the sample had chronic reference theft. The problem occurred over 20 times in 14% of the institutions. Overall, the rate of reference theft was 740.

> Attempts to remove reference materials and attempts to sneak out of the reference library through the rear exit have been problems.

Audio-visual materials. Access to AV items tends to be more closely controlled than is access to books and reference materials. This is reflected in the level of theft of AV materials and equipment. Two thirds of the returns indicated no known episodes of stolen AV materials. An additional 9% had only one or two AV thefts. Just over 15% had chronic AV theft. The highest reported level of AV theft, over 20 times, occurred in 8% of the cases. The rate per 100 of AV theft was 339.

> The theft of casettes is a serious problem in our library. A locked display has greatly reduced this problem.

Book and nonbook resources. How serious is the problem of theft of library resources? Combining the items related to book theft, reference material theft, and AV material theft provides a rough estimate of the losses of book and nonbook resources. Only 8% of the libraries had no known occurrences of resource theft. One quarter reported 8 or fewer episodes. Half of the libraries had more than 26 separate occurrences of theft of resources. Nearly 15% of the sample had more than 50 repetitions. Once again, responses of "over 20" were counted as 25. For every 100 libraries there were over 2750 thefts of book and nonbook resources.

Equipment. A general question was asked about the theft of equipment. Since no specific types of equipment were specified, responses to this item would indicate the loss of AV equipment (cameras, tape recorders, televisions, and so on) as well as photocopying machines, computers and accessories, office equipment, maintenance equipment and so on. The theft of equipment was chronic in only 5% of the cases. The majority of responses (59%) reported no such thefts. An additional 30% had only one or two episodes during the year. The average number of equipment thefts was 1.7.

Fraudulent billing. The thefts described above all involve materials being taken directly from the library or library grounds. Various physical security procedures may be effective in reducing the occurrence of those episodes. If professionals attempt to defraud the library by billing for nonexistent materials, by overbilling or duplicating bills, then different types of security issues are involved. The success of fraudulent billing depends upon the phony transactions not being detected. This implies that we are being told only of those cases in which detection was made—the unsuccessful cases. It appears that fraudulent billing is a crime that tends to be repeated against the unsuspecting library. While only 9% of the returns mentioned a case of fraudulent billing, the vast majority of these cases were repeated. That is, 91% had no known attempts, 2% reported one episode, 3% knew of 2 attempts, and an additional 4% indicated over 2 cases. When phony billing occurs once, it is likely to reoccur until detected. The fraudulent billing rate was 32.

Counterfeit money. The repeated exchange or use of counterfeit money is a crime most likely to be carried out by professionals. Access to large amounts of counterfeit money requires a certain amount of expertise and criminal contacts. Successful use of counterfeit cash requires a victim incapable of or too busy to identify the bogus notes. Making an exchange in a busy public building such as a department store, theater, market, or library may be a favored procedure. Nearly 1 of 10 libraries were aware of someone's passing counterfeit bills. Many more probably never knew that attempts had occurred. Once again, when one episode had occurred, multiple cases were the norm. Among those libraries that had at least one problem with counterfeit money, nearly 90% had repeated cases. There were 60 reported cases in each 100 libraries.

Personal property. Thousands of thefts of library property were found in the sample of Great Britain's libraries. In addition, patrons and staff may have been victims of theft of their own property. Over half (57%) of the sample reported that the theft of personal property did occur. Many of these cases involved only one or two known thefts (44%). Five percent of the libraries had experienced 6 or more personal property thefts. However, it is likely that many thefts went unnoticed (cash from pocket books that was presumed lost or stolen in some other setting, etc.) or not reported to library personnel. The personal property theft rate was 156.

Other theft. Since it was impossible to anticipate all the different kinds of items that could be stolen from a public library, a catch-all category of "other theft" was included. This means that in addition to the reported thefts of books, reference materials, personal property and so on, additional thefts had occurred. The majority of respondents reported at least one additional theft. Approximately one third of the institutions suffered one or two other thefts. One in ten libraries knew of 6 or more other thefts.

Breaking and entering. Not all cases of illegal entry resulted in successful theft. Some were precursors to acts of vandalism, while others involved no additional crime. However, illegal entry into the library often preceded theft. Therefore, we have included breaking and entering along with descriptions of the different kinds of theft. Unlike some of the more secretive crimes, illegal entry is usually detectable. Forced entry into the library was found in under half of the sample. Just over 25% reported one or two episodes, and 10% had 3-5 repetitions. Only 5% suffered chronic breaking and entering. Each episode of breaking and entering probably included other loss or damage, and thus the impact of illegal entry extends beyond any damage to the door or window itself. The break-in rate was 136.

> Petty thefts following break-ins at HQ have resulted in a real nuisance rather than great loss or damage. In fact the local thieves appear to treat our book stock and equipment with great respect.

Theft index. The nine different theft items were combined to form an index measuring the total problem with theft. It is interesting to note that only 3% of the sample was free from theft of any kind. One quarter of those reporting had 12 or fewer thefts during the year. An additional quarter had between 12 and 32 thefts. Over 50 known thefts per year were experienced by one third of all libraries. Examination of the frequency of theft shows that the average number of separate episodes of theft reported by each library in the sample was 35 per year. In other words the overall reported rate of theft was 3500 incidents for every 100 libraries.

Problem Patrons

Any behavior that disrupts the library could be considered "problem patron behavior." This would include many of the criminal behaviors already described—book theft, arson, vandalism, etc. However, for our purposes, and to be consistent with the typical treatment of the problem patron in other studies, problem patron behavior includes actions that are likely to be considered offensive to staff or patrons. The term "offensive" is a relative term. What is offensive to one library administrator may be considered simply a nuisance to another. Although the term lacks scientific precision, it probably reflects what it is supposed to reflect—behaviors defined as a problem in the local setting. Some of the actions may not be crimes as in the case of rude and noisy or offensively dressed and unbathed patrons. Other problems, such as drug use and sales or indecent exposure, would be in violation of law.

> Groups of youth (female and male) congregating (up to 12 in one group) cause tension in staff and other users even when groups are not misbehaving. Frequently, the behavior becomes completely unacceptable (physical horseplay, as opposed to violence, and the noise level.)

> Our problem is turning 'gentlemen of the road' out at closing time.

Altogether, six specific problem patron behaviors were investigated. Two of these, drug use and drug sales are likely to be practiced in secrecy and, unless observed by a staff member happening on the scene, would not be reported to us. The others including verbal abuse, obscene phone calls and indecent exposure are public offenses by their very nature. The reports of the latter problems are more likely to be accurate estimates.

Drug use and sales. The use of the library as a setting for drug use appears to be an all or nothing problem. This is not an unexpected finding. Juveniles and/or adults using drugs tend to search for "safe" settings. Once an appropriate location is found, it may become defined as a meeting place for use and sales. If that favored location comes under surveillance, then a new setting will be chosen. Responses from the surveys indicate that alcohol problems and "drunks" were considered separately from the problems of drug use and sales. In this study most libraries (88%) reportedly were free of drug use by staff or patrons. This implies that even if drug use was occurring but was undetected, it was not interfering with the routine functioning of the facility. In the libraries where drug use was noticed, roughly half of the cases involved one or two episodes, while the other half had a repeated problem. As many libraries had more than 10 known cases as had only a single violation.

> Teenagers, some of whom, unfortunately are resorting to glue sniffing before coming into the library and after they get there. The problem seems to be increasing each year.

> We see quite a bit of drug use of the cough mixture variety — sometimes within the library (bottles found etc.) We experience little difficulty with the users. The worst problem is drunkenness, which appears to be increasing locally.

Drug sales in the library were rare. However, once again we see the pattern of repetition. Only four libraries reportedly had ongoing drug sales. Three of these reported 6-10 repetitions, while the final respondent knew of 11-15 cases. The rate of drug use was 80, and was higher than that for drug sales (20/100).

Verbal abuse to patrons. Most patrons anticipate that their library will be a safe and comfortable place to be. Those that think otherwise are less likely to actually use the library. Verbal abuse of a patron occurred in over half of the responding libraries. When it did occur, it tended to be a repeated form of disruption. For example, less than 10% of the reports indicated only one episode, while 26% had 2-5 cases. Nearly 10% of the returns mentioned that there were more than 10 cases during the year. Overall, there were 3.3 cases per year in the average library or 330 known episodes per 100 libraries.

> We have regular visits from 'gangs' of, usually, young boys who subject the patrons to abuse and on some occasions threats of violence.

> We have little problem with intentional crime. However, we do attract a very small minority of mentally disturbed people who can be disruptive. They tend to disturb other users enjoyment of the library.

Verbal abuse to staff. The likelihood of a staff member's being verbally abused was among the highest of the 24 problems studied Exactly three quarters of our respondents mentioned verbal abuse of a staff member. Almost all of these cases tended to be recurring problems. Only 10% of the sample had single cases. Nearly one third of the libraries had 3-10 known abuses, while 23% had over 10 repetitions. The typical library had 6.7 cases per year (670/100). Later in this chapter it will be shown that despite the fact that verbal abuse was not among the most dangerous or costly offenses, it is perceived to be among the most disruptive and unsettling to the library and its staff.

> Most of our problems are caused by young teenagers between 6 and 10 p.m. Most of our libraries are in the centre of town. The behavior is mostly hooliganism and verbal abuse when remonstrated with.

> Groups of youth disrupt the service on dark evenings, either by banging on windows from outside or coming inside and shouting at us and harassing the staff (usually when all female staff are on duty).

> The most serious problem is threats to staff between 6-8 p.m.

Obscene phone calls. Whereas patrons and staff may be verbally abused in a face to face situation, the staff also may experience obscene phone calls made to the library. Most libraries apparently were free from this problem. Only 26% of respondents knew of obscene phone calls. Among this group, most had repeated problems. Only 4% had more than 10 calls per year, but 13% had two or more. The definition of an obscene phone call was left to the respondent. Whether a particular phone call had any "redeeming social value" or was obscene probably varied from place to place. It is estimated that the annual rate of obscene calls was 131 per 100 libraries.

Indecent exposure. Perhaps the most unsettling of the problem patron behaviors is indecent exposure. It was not a common problem. Just under 15% of the returns mentioned having at least one case. Half of those libraries had only a single problem, while the remaining half had two or more.

Problem patron index. Nearly all of the surveys returned mentioned having some kind of problem with patrons. About one tenth had only a single episode, while 75% had two or more cases. The average number of problem patron disruptions was 12 per year (1200/100). In some libraries, dealing with these was almost a regular problem. One of 20 libraries reported having over 50 instances during the year in question.

Assault

Assault against patrons. The crime that tends to instill the greatest fear is that of assault. This fear persists despite the fact that assaults are among the least likely crimes to occur. This is true in Great Britain's libraries as well. Less than 10% of the surveys mentioned an assault against a patron. This was limited to a single assault in half of these cases. Only 1 library reported more than 10 assaults in the year in question. The rate of assault against a patron was 23/100 libraries.

> Our most serious type of problem occurred recently with a child who had an airgun who was taking shots at our windows and at patrons going into the library.

Assault against staff. Library staff were somewhat more likely than patrons to be victims of an assault at the library. An assault against staff occurred in about 1 of 7 libraries. Once again most of these were single episodes, but 5% had two or more incidents. Only one library had more than 5 assaults. The rate of assault against staff was 27/100.

> One isolated, yet serious, incident was the shooting of an air

rifle pellet through a rear library window, narrowly missing the caretaker.

Assault index. When the two assault items are combined it appears than nearly one fifth of the sample (17%) knew of at least one assault against either a staff member or a patron. Only two libraries reported more than 10 assaults. The majority of the victimizations were single cases. The overall assault rate was 49 reported cases for every 100 libraries.

Total crime and disruption. If all 24 types of crime and disruption are considered together, then virtually all libraries have some problems. It is the unusual library that is completely free of all crime. In fact only 3% of the respondents reported 2 or less episodes. More than half of the sample had over 50 known cases of crime and disruption. There were at least 100 known offenses in 25% of the sampled libraries. The estimated rate of total offenses is staggering. For every 100 libraries there were reportedly 6,922 separate offenses—an average of 69 in each library. This far surpasses the official rates of offense recorded for Great Britain (less than 5,000/100,000 people). It is worth repeating that these estimates will tend to be conservative in part because not all offenses were known to our respondents and some that were may not have been reported to us. It also should be pointed out that the Total Index and other indices exclude cases with any missing data. That is, if any of the questions about theft were omitted, then the theft index does not include that library's response. Moreover, since the indices do not always include exactly the same libraries, the Total Index is not always equal to the sum of the other indices.

PERSONAL VICTIMIZATION

The discussion so far has centered on crimes that occurred within a one-year period in the sampled libraries. This is a good way to determine annual rates of crime and to establish an understanding of the patterns of crime. There is another interesting question that can be asked about crime. What patterns emerge if respondents are asked if crime ever occurred? Obviously there are problems of recall, staffing changes, and record keeping. Thus we chose not to develop this avenue in any detail. However, it is possible to get reliable estimates of personal victimization in this way. The exact date and some details of the victimization may be blurred, but most victims do remember how many times they have been victimized.

We asked the respondent: "Have you been the victim of a personal crime or crime against your property while in the library?" The majority of respondents (59%) answered that they had not. Just under a fourth had been victimized once while in the library. Eleven percent of the respondents mentioned two instances of personal victimization, and 6% reported three or more cases. Were men or women more likely to be victims of crime in the library? It appears that there are differences. Forty-four percent of the males reported at least one victimization compared with 35% of the women. However, women were three times as likely to be victimized more than twice (9% vs. 3%).

INSTITUTIONAL FACTORS RELATED TO CRIME

Crime does not occur in isolation from social and environmental conditions. The patterns of crime found in the sample of Great Britain's libraries have been described in detail. Now it is time to develop some understanding of what influences these patterns. Questions on several institutional factors were included in the survey. These included the number of patrons served, annual circulation, and staff size. Certainly other institutional conditions, such as the physical arrangement of the building, might influence crime. In addition, the use of various security devices and programs was examined in detail, and this is described fully in Chapter 5. At that time the relationship between security use and the level and patterns of crime will be examined.

Number of patrons. As mentioned earlier, the number of patrons served is an indicator of the activity level of the library. There are two hypotheses that might be offered about the relationship between the level of activity and the level of crime. The first suggests that the busier the library, the greater the opportunity for crime. The argument here is that the more people there are in and around the library, the greater the number of potential victims and offenders. Busy libraries also may have more difficulty keeping proper checks on the behavior of their patrons. Further, the staff are less likely to be able to identify all or most of the patrons, a condition that fosters feelings of anonymity. The belief that identification is difficult or impossible facilitates the committing of crimes. The competing hypothesis suggests that the less active the library, the greater the possibility of committing a crime without being seen. The reasoning here is that libraries that have few patrons afford potential offenders the chance to commit crimes without there being any witnesses. In other words, the presence of other people acts as a deterrent to crime. It is, of course, possible that both hypotheses are accurate, but for different types of crime.

As a first step in examining the possible relationship between the number of patrons and the level of crime, the correlations between the variables were computed. Basically, a correlation examines the strength of the relationship between two (or more) variables. A positive correlation indicates that the two variables, in this case the number of patrons and the level of crime, change in the same direction. As the number of patrons increases the level of crime also increases. A negative correlation indicates that the two variables are changing in opposite directions, i.e., as the number of patrons increases the level of crime decreases.

In most cases there is a positive relationship between the number of patrons who use the library on a daily basis and the level of crime. A correlation is considered significant if there is less than a 5% probability that it could occur by chance. Using this criteria, most of the 24 crime items are positively correlated with the number of patrons. However, the strength of this relationship varies. The theft of reference material is the crime most highly correlated with the number of patrons ($r. = .50$). This would suggest that the increased demand for valued reference materials overrides the possible deterrent effect of the theft's being observed by another patron. Another possibility is that, even if observed, other patrons are not likely to take action to stop or report the offender. This is consistent with the findings of several studies including Hoppe and Simmel (1969). A strong relationship ($r. = .40$) also was found between the theft of personal property and the number of patrons. This provides direct support for theories that suggest that theft often is a crime of opportunity. The more patrons in the library, the more personal belongings there may be left unguarded.

As can be seen in Table 2.8, several other crime items showed strong relationships with the level of patron use. Book theft was highly correlated with the number of patrons, as was intentional damage to books. Both of these offenses may be symptoms of *perceived* shortages of resources. As pressure to gain access to valued materials increases, patrons may start to use illegitimate means to

Table 2.8

Correlations of Crime Items with Institutional Factors and City Size

Type of Episode	# Patrons	Circulation	City Size
Book damage	.26	.23	.36
Vandalism outside	.10	.14	.28
Vandalism inside	.18	.13	.13
Equipment damage	.23	.16	.03
Damage staff car	-.02	-.11	-.01
Damage patron car	.09	.03	.09
Arson	.10	-.05	.10
Book theft	.31	.34	.38
Reference theft	.50	.37	.24
A V theft	.23	.24	.14
Equipment theft	.15	.17	.17
Fraudulent bill	.14	.13	.07
Counterfeit money	.05	.06	-.04
Personal theft	.40	.29	.27
Other theft	.23	.09	.19
Forced entry	.19	.13	.22
Drug use	.14	.12	.14
Drug sales	.15	-.03	.06
Harassed patron	.18	.20	.28
Harassed staff	.16	.07	.27
Obscene calls	.09	.09	.23
Indecent exposure	.17	.13	.20
Assault on patron	.21	.16	.19
Assault on staff	.28	.08	.23
INDICES:			
Vandalism	.21	.23	.30
Theft	.48	.39	.38
Problem Patron	.15	.13	.31
Assault	.22	.12	.16
Total	.34	.32	.39

$r=.12$ $(p<.05)$
$r=.16$ $(p<.01)$
$r=.22$ $(p<.001)$

get what they want. Assault against staff members was another highly correlated crime. Most remaining items also were significantly correlated with the number of patrons. However, a few problems did not increase as the number of patrons increased. These included vandalism to staff and patron owned cars, vandalism outside the building, passing bogus money, and obscene phone calls. The three vandalism items, all involving problems outside the building, might be deterred by the arrival of patrons constantly entering the building. Also, vandalism inside the building did not increase as patrons increased, suggesting a deterrent effect for nonacquisitive vandalism. A person making obscene phone calls would not be affected by the number of patrons in the building since an audience of one is sufficient.

The second way to examine the relationship between these two variables is to compare the average scores for each crime item as a function of the number of patrons in the library. That is, how much book theft is there in libraries serving 100 patrons compared with libraries serving 1,000 patrons. Most, but not all crimes, occur more frequently when there are more rather than fewer patrons in the building. Table 2.9 provides the average number of incidences of each crime for libraries serving different numbers of patrons. In some cases there is an increase in the average level of crime for each increase in the number of patrons using the library. This is true of reference theft, indecent exposure, assault against staff, arson and personal property theft. To illustrate, reference theft occurred an average of two times in libraries reporting 51-100 patrons daily, 3 times with 101-250 patrons, nearly 7 times with 251-500 patrons, 11 times annually with 501-1,000 patrons, and an average of 13 times with over 1,000 patrons.

Other crimes show increases in frequency up to a certain level of patron use, but then level off as more patrons appear. Here we find book damage, book theft and AV theft, which increase until 500-1,000 patrons are present, and then decline. Other offenses exhibit a general increase as the number of patrons rises, but the pattern is imperfect. For example, a decline at a middle level of patron use can be followed by additional increases. Examples include equipment theft, other theft, drug use, vandalism to patrons' cars, equipment vandalism and assault against patrons. Finally, the frequency of some offenses are not related systematically to an increase in the number of patrons. Included here are vandalism outside the building, vandalism to staff cars, verbal abuse to staff, breaking and entering, fraudulent billing, and obscene phone calls.

Circulation level. The second item having to do with the activity level of the library also appears to bear a relationship to the amount of crime in the library. The strongest correlations are found between the circulation level and the theft of reference material (r. = .37), followed by book theft (r. = .34), personal property theft (r. = .29), AV theft (r. = .24) and intentional book damage (r. = .23).

Table 2.9

Crime Rates as a Function of Patron Activity Level

Type of Episode	Number of Patrons in 100s					
	<.5	.5-1	1-2.5	2.5-5	5-10	+10
Book damage	250	686	675	983	1,594	1,009
Vandalism outside	275	593	458	643	472	733
Vandalism inside	25	350	230	300	474	503
Equipment damage	0	107	14	114	134	166
Damage staff car	25	47	33	16	47	23
Damage patron car	0	21	18	22	27	120
Arson	25	0	13	20	28	27
Book theft	200	885	1,393	1,964	2,005	1,856
Reference theft	25	200	300	668	1,105	1,310
A V theft	0	167	166	453	519	376
Equipment theft	0	73	144	127	213	266
Fraudulent bill	0	0	20	47	18	59
Counterfeit money	0	33	47	29	122	74
Personal theft	25	40	55	104	185	363
Other theft	50	43	171	428	303	408
Forced entry	50	87	69	120	75	263
Drug use	0	27	60	57	71	174
Drug sales	0	0	0	0	41	56
Harassed patron	25	227	186	438	439	369
Harassed staff	50	567	480	760	913	688
Obscene calls	50	167	78	135	66	198
Indecent exposure	0	7	11	35	61	85
Assault on patron	0	0	2	14	10	80
Assault on staff	0	0	9	12	23	83
INDICES:						
Vandalism	333	2,063	1,421	2,096	2,691	2,441
Theft	350	1,458	2,266	3,880	4,552	5,093
Problem Patron	125	993	826	1,478	1,583	1,367
Assault	0	0	9	27	34	163
Total	700	4,056	4,777	7,886	8,719	8,696

Several crime items were not systematically related to the circulation level at a statistically significant level (p = .05). These included other theft, vandalism to staff and patrons' cars, verbal abuse to staff, assault against staff, arson and obscene phone calls (See Table 2.8). Annual circulation was significantly related to several of the indices, including Theft (r. = .39) Vandalism (r. = .23) and the Total index (r. = .32).

The correlations between many of the crime items and the level of circulation show that in general the incidence of crime is greater when circulation is higher. In fact, some of the crimes only occurred in libraries with relatively high levels of circulation. For example, there was no drug use, indecent exposure, assault against patron, or fraudulent billing in libraries circulating less than 50,000 items. In some cases, such as breaking and entering, personal property theft, equipment theft and reference theft, the rates of crime were several times higher for libraries circulating over 500,000 items than for any other libraries.

Staff size. The number of professional librarians was positively correlated with 18 of the 24 crime items. The strongest associations were found with the theft of personal property (r. = .59), reference theft (r. = .47), breaking and entering (r. = .34), and assault against patron and staff (both r. = .30). Most other types of vandalism and theft also were significantly correlated with the size of the professional staff. Damage to cars, drug use, indecent exposure, arson and passing counterfeit money were not related to staff size. Similar patterns appeared when the relationship between the number of nonprofessionals and levels of crime were examined.

The relationship between using security personnel and the level of crime is more complex. It would be expected that the use of security staff would lower the crime rate. This suggests that negative correlations might be found. That is, as the number of security personnel increases the average level of crime decreases. This was not the case. None of the 24 crime items showed a significant negative correlation with the size of the security staff. However, assaults against staff, arson and passing counterfeit money showed a trend in this direction. It appears that these more serious crimes do decline somewhat as security personnel increase. The important question, however, is whether the crime rate would be even higher without security personnel. Most security staff are added to the payroll when problems already are at serious levels. These relationships will be examined in more detail in Chapter 5.

SITUATIONAL FACTORS

One of the consistent findings from a variety of studies on crime patterns is that major differences appear as a function of city size. These differences often are so striking that it is important to control for city size when doing comparative studies of crime. In this study, the size of the city in which the library was located was strongly related to the level of different kinds of theft and most forms of problem patron behavior. For example, there were strong correlations between city size and the rates of book theft (r. = .36), book damage (r. = .38), verbal abuse to patron (r. = .28) and verbal abuse to staff (r. = .27). It was not as strongly associated with the types of vandalism occurring outside the library. Rather, this type of vandalism tended to increase from smaller to middle size cities, and then drop somewhat in the largest cities. One possible interpretation is that librarians working in the largest cities do not respond to vandalism in the same way that others do. If vandalism to public buildings is an everyday event, then minor incidents affecting the library may be ignored and not reported to us. On the other hand, larger cities may have more police visibility, which would act as a deterrent to acts of vandalism.

The average number of reported crimes increased dramatically as population increased. These patterns are shown in Table 2.10. For several crimes, including book damage and theft, verbal abuse and assault against staff, there were steady increases. To illustrate, the average number of book thefts in towns under 10,000 was 5.2. In towns between 10,000 and 50,000 there were almost 17 episodes per library, the number rose to 19 in cities of 50,000-100,000 and then continued to increase as city size increased.

Controlling for city size. What happens to the relationship between the number of patrons or circulation level and the level of crime if city size is controlled. In other words, if the number of patrons is examined only in cities of the same size, is the number still an important factor? Computing second order correlations examines just this issue. We find that book theft, reference theft and personal theft still are strongly related to the number of patrons using the library. Most of the other crimes are not as closely related to patron activity level. In cities of comparable size, the circulation level was most closely related to the level of book theft and reference theft.

National variations. Earlier we discussed some of the difficulties in comparing crime across national boundaries. It should be pointed out again that the comparisons in this study involve the larger district and central libraries, not a representative sampling of each nation's libraries. England (140) and Scotland (43) are well represented in the sample, while there are only 20 libraries from Wales among the returned surveys. What can be said with certainty is that, within this sample, the country with the highest rate of crime varied, depending on the type of crime in question.

Table 2.10

Crime Rates per 100 Libraries as a Function of City Size

Type of Episode	City Size in 1,000s				
	2.5-10	10-50	50-100	100-500	+500
Book damage	370	852	1,132	1,205	1,393
Vandalism outside	290	394	570	828	788
Vandalism inside	143	402	245	472	244
Equipment damage	84	96	110	119	36
Damage staff car	38	25	39	38	6
Damage patron car	9	25	16	94	6
Arson	0	19	26	28	13
Book theft	524	1,659	1,890	1,907	2,100
Reference theft	214	621	982	973	806
A V theft	0	412	445	278	773
Equipment theft	38	77	283	259	119
Fraudulent bill	5	33	65	33	25
Counterfeit money	19	87	16	90	0
Personal theft	20	78	269	181	338
Other theft	114	265	120	439	427
Forced entry	33	87	83	207	269
Drug use	0	25	10	196	13
Drug sales	0	0	52	34	0
Harassed patron	95	221	252	457	781
Harassed staff	486	539	510	933	838
Obscene calls	52	70	30	220	330
Indecent exposure	10	26	10	59	138
Assault on patron	0	4	3	50	31
Assault on staff	0	13	13	49	56
INDICES:					
Vandalism	936	1,756	2,136	2,762	2,593
Theft	1,025	3,250	4,217	4,280	4,786
Problem Patron	643	838	861	1,797	2,094
Assault	0	17	17	95	88
Total	2,547	5,957	7,495	9,082	9,046

With this in mind there are some noteworthy differences. English libraries showed the highest crime rates for book damage, book theft, equipment theft, other theft, vandalism to equipment, verbal abuse to patrons, indecent exposure, assault against patrons, arson, counterfeit passing and fraudulent billing. Welsh libraries demonstrated the highest rates of inside and outside vandalism, drug use, breaking and entering, theft of personal property, AV theft and obscene phone calls. The Scottish libraries in the sample were highest only for vandalism to staff and patron cars (see Table 2.11). These variations in peak crime rates occur despite the fact that the average English library was busier and located in a larger city.

COSTS OF CRIME

A detailed description of crime patterns provides one kind of information that is useful to those working to control crime in the

Table 2.11

Library Crime Rates/100 in England, Scotland and Wales

Type of Episode	England	Scotland	Wales
Book damage	1,104	681	836
Vandalism outside	638	310	800
Vandalism inside	368	225	436
Equipment damage	131	32	71
Damage staff car	28	49	14
Damage patron car	48	46	14
Arson	27	5	14
Book theft	1,841	1,219	1,392
Reference theft	850	375	738
A V theft	350	310	379
Equipment theft	205	39	43
Fraudulent bill	43	15	14
Counterfeit money	86	10	0
Personal theft	177	78	207
Other theft	368	171	118
Forced entry	141	50	357
Drug use	93	12	200
Drug sales	29	0	0
Harassed patron	382	224	150
Harassed staff	708	439	971
Obscene calls	119	132	357
Indecent exposure	50	30	14
Assault on patron	33	0	7
Assault on staff	31	10	21
INDICES:			
Vandalism	2,347	1,265	2,186
Theft	4,016	2,285	2,955
Problem Patron	1,323	843	1,693
Assault	63	10	29
Total	8,080	4,154	6,573

library. What is lacking in this kind of statistical analysis is a sense of how crime affects patrons, staff and the institution. Every criminal act has consequences for those involved. The severity of the consequences depends in part on whether one is the actual victim of the crime, personally involved with the victim, or merely an observer. Crimes directed against public institutions such as libraries tend to affect a number of people but in different ways. Staff may be concerned about their safety and about the ability to maintain the mission of the library. Patrons may be concerned about the level of services and availability of resources in addition to their safety. Some of the costs of crime are short term. The theft of a small amount of money from a purse may be a short term problem. On the other hand, if a purse containing money, license, credit cards, treasured photographs, etc., is stolen then the costs of crime may be more long term. Months may pass before all the cards are replaced. The disappointment over losing the photos may linger forever. Changes in personal behavior and attitudes, such as never feeling safe in the library again, are other possible long term costs. Even minor crimes may have serious longterm impacts. More serious crimes are particularly likely to involve both short and long term costs.

Institutional Costs

Financial cost. The financial loss due to crime is not the best indicator of the severity of crime, but it is one of the easiest to measure. Respondents were asked to estimate the total losses due to crime and disruption during the previous year. As shown in Table 2.12, a few (4%) libraries reported no losses. However, it was much more typical to have significant losses due to crime. Over half (60%) of the sample had losses exceeding 250 pounds, and 24% had losses over 2,500 pounds. Twelve percent of the sample experienced at least a 5,000 pound loss. Many respondents indicated that they reported a loss only when the damage had been repaired or the loss had been replaced during the year in question. Recall that, for the libraries responding to the question, the average number of stolen books and journals was over 250. If each institution replaced all of the missing items the actual average losses just for these items would approach 5,000 pounds.

Crime prevention expenses. When crime occurs, there are some costs that are the direct result of a particular crime such as money

Table 2.12
Crime Loss and Prevention Costs

	% Reporting			
	England	Scotland	Wales	Total
Crime Losses				
None	2	8	8	4
<50 (pounds)	8	28	8	13
51-100	9	15	8	10
101-250	14	8	23	13
251-500	12	8	15	12
501-1,000	12	13	23	13
1,001-2,500	12	15	15	13
2,501-5,000	16	3	0	12
>5,000	14	3	0	11
Security Expenses				
None	45	58	50	49
<50 (pounds)	10	8	7	9
51-100	7	5	7	6
101-250	4	5	0	4
251-500	8	3	21	8
501-1,000	10	10	7	10
1,001-2,500	3	0	0	2
2,501-5,000	4	5	0	4
>5,000	9	5	7	8

lost, equipment stolen, repairs necessitated and so on. Other costs are incurred because there is the anticipation of subsequent crime. The development of security programs and the installation of security devices are good examples of costs related to the anticipation of crime. Chapter 5 focuses on these security measures. Here we will briefly examine the annual cost involved in the implementing of security measures. Exactly 50% of returns mentioned no crime prevention expenditures, despite the fact that there were problems with crime and disruption. Of the remaining libraries, half spent less than 500 pounds and half spent more. Less than 10% of the sample reportedly spent over 5,000 pounds during the year (see Table 2.12).

Total expenses. An estimate of the expenses resulting from crime can be obtained by adding together the reported losses and reported crime prevention expenditures. Less than 5% claimed that they incurred no expenses related to crime, while expenses of more than

5,000 pounds were incurred by 19% of the sample. Just 5% of the returns indicated total costs over 10,000 pounds.

Closed the library. Do problems with crime ever become so serious that a decision is made to close the library? In some of the cases reported to us libraries were closed. Many of the closings were the result of extensive damage from arson and occasionally vandalism. Eleven libraries in the sample (5%) closed at least once. Only two libraries closed three or more times. The rate of closing was 9 times for each 100 libraries. Buildings were most likely to be closed when there were high levels of drug use and drug sales, breaking and entering, arson, and personal property thefts. Since the sample included central and district libraries, it was possible to ask if a branch was ever closed down because of crime. Eight percent of the responses mentioned that a branch had to be closed. Most of these involved a single closing. Table 2.13 contains the *rates* of institutional responses to crime. As shown, Welsh libraries were more likely to experience a forced closing.

Changed schedule. A less drastic response to crime is to alter the operating hours. Nearly 1 of 10 libraries reportedly changed their

Table 2.13

Personal and Institutional Effects of Crime

	Rate per 100 Libraries			
Institutional Impact	England	Scotland	Wales	Total
Closed library	12	0	15	9
Closed branch library	12	5	15	11
Changed operating hours	13	2	21	11
Lost use of equipment	25	0	8	18
Stopped community programs	12	0	0	8
Called police	210	169	200	200
Training session	36	12	29	30
Staff Impact	Proportion Reporting			
Avoid work after dark	18	0	8	14
Picked up after work	19	15	21	18
Escorted to car	22	7	15	18

open hours in an attempt to deal with problems of crime and safety. Several libraries changed their schedule more than once as they tried to find the most appropriate schedule. Changes for reasons other than crime problems (budget, vacation periods, etc.) are not included here. Choosing to change the schedule was strongly correlated with several crime problems, including outside vandalism, drug use and sales, assaults, arson, breaking and entering and personal property thefts. Once again, libraries in Wales were more likely to initiate schedule changes.

> If this questionnaire had covered the last 18 months rather than the last 12 months, some of the answers would have been very different. The library hours were changed to only day time ones as a direct result of hooliganism after dark, when the library was open. Since the change of hours there has been no trouble at all.

> In one case we had to alter operating hours and increase staff presence to try to control the problems.

Lost use of equipment. As a result of theft or vandalism some equipment may be lost temporarily or permanently. These losses produce an impact upon both staff and public. Over 10% of the returns indicated that equipment was lost at least once. Three percent reportedly lost the use of equipment 3 or more times during the year. Libraries that lost the use of equipment also had high levels of drug sales and assaults in the library along with theft and destruction of the equipment. English libraries were the most likely to report the loss of equipment.

Stopped programs. Acts of crime often spill over to affect those who were not involved in any way initially. This is what happens when programs for the community are stopped because of crime. Just over 5% of the cases had programs discontinued. These cases occurred only in English libraries. Stopping a community program was strongly correlated with drug sales, arson and assault against a staff member.

Calling the police. The most common response to crime is to call the police. Approximately three quarters of the sample had called the police during the year. Exactly one third had called only once or twice. Forty percent of the cases involved repeated calls. Nearly 10% called more than 10 times. The average number of annual calls to the police was over two per year. While all the crime items were related to calling the police, the decision to call was most strongly correlated with verbal abuse to the staff and patrons, vandalism inside and outside the building and breaking and entering. Notice that only breaking and entering usually is classified as a serious crime. Verbal abuse showed the strongest relationship with calling the police. This is an indication that the way staff are treated by patrons is a significant factor in their perceptions of safety and wellbeing in the library. Outside help usually is sought when staff feel that they cannot, or should not have to, handle the situation alone.

> Alcoholics and 'down and outs' frequent my library. Generally if they will not leave the building quietly, a phone call to the police is usually sufficient to frighten them off. We very rarely have to prosecute them.

> Aggressive, drunken and violent behavior which creates disturbances and causes fear in the minds of the staff is reduced by regular calls to and visits from a uniformed police officer — say 3 times a week.

Effect on services. Respondents were asked for their opinion on how much crime and disruption affected services to the public. A small group (13%) indicated that there was no effect at all. The most common response (59%) was that crime affected services "very little." Approximately one in five libraries were affected moderately, and 5% a great deal. A perceived strong effect on services to the public was most closely associated with high levels of verbal abuse to patrons and staff, book damage, book theft, drug use and vandalism inside the building.

> The suspected high volume of book theft must reduce service to the public. We just don't have all the figures.

> Fear of crime from large teenagers roaming the area at night keeps most of the population (elderly) indoors at night. Our service is underused after 5 P.M. and even earlier in the winter.

National differences. The impact of crime on libraries was greatest in England. This was true for total financial losses as well as for the overall institutional responses to crime. Consistent with the findings on the frequency of crime, the impact of crime was perceived to be the lowest by the Scottish respondents.

Personal Costs

So far the impact of crime on the institution has been the focus. There is no doubt that crime can affect the budget, services, and resources of a library. The other important consideration is how crime affects the behavior and attitudes of those working in the library. There were five indicators of personal behavior changes that may have occurred because of apprehension about crime. These included avoiding work at selected times and taking special precautions when leaving the building.

Work avoidance. It is not uncommon for people who fear becoming victims in their workplace to avoid work at times. This has been shown in studies of school crime conducted in the United States. Teachers and students in high risk schools reported absenteeism that resulted from a fear of crime. We asked about less dramatic behavior—avoiding work after dark. Among the actual respondents, 14% reported that they personally avoided working after dark because of a fear of crime. Males were more likely than females to do so. Ten percent knew of other staff members asking not to work after dark. Avoiding work after dark was most closely related to the level of indecent exposure, vandalism to cars, arson and verbal abuse.

Fear of isolation. Being alone in a dangerous location or situation is a major concern among those wary of crime. One such critical time would be when leaving the facility. In one of six libraries surveyed there are procedures to escort staff to their cars or out of the building at the close of work. Eighteen percent of the returns indicated that the respondent was picked up by someone after work because of concerns about crime. There were no differences between male and female employees. Escorting staff out of the building was related to high levels of drug sales, vandalism outside the library, assault, arson and verbal abuse.

> The harassment of staff by mainly groups of teenage hooligans has caused us to employ extra staff to ensure that there were always 2 people working in the evenings.

Training. Traditionally, librarians and other public administrators have not been trained in crime prevention and security. Many institutions have been using staff workshops and training sessions as institutions have been using staff workshops and training sessions as a way of filling this need. Nearly a third (30%) of the libraries surveyed did have crime prevention or security training sessions for their staff. Training sessions were most likely to be instituted in libaries with high levels of personal thefts, verbal abuse, book and reference theft, book damage and vandalism inside the building. The correlation between having training sessions and the total level of crime also was highly significant.

> The library is used as a general meeting place by all sections of the community which we welcome, but this does result in unruly behavior at times. Many seminars and discussions on disruptions and hooliganism in libraries have been held and advice sought from police and social services staff. None have found any real answers. It appears to be a fact of modern life that staff must learn to live with.

Personal impact. Examination of the five items related to personal costs shows that approximately half (46%) of the respondents took some action because of crime. One fifth knew of two or more of the responses occurring in their library. As concerns about crime and safety may interfere with the quality of the work setting and performance of library personnel, steps should be taken to deal with these concerns.

SUMMARY

Three hundred central and district libraries were sampled, resulting in over 200 returns.

Crime patterns in Britain's public libraries were not unlike the general patterns of crime found throughout the society in that the most common library crimes involved theft and vandalism.

Drug sales, arson, assaults on patrons and assaults on staff were the crimes least likely to occur.

The rate of theft was approximately 3,500 per 100 libraries. The total rate of crime, nearly 7,000/100, far surpassed the rate of crime officially reported for Great Britain.

Library crime patterns were related to both the levels of circulation and patron activity.

Virtually all libraries reported some problems with crime and disruption.

As city size increased, the level of crime tended to increase. However the relationship was not perfect. Some crimes, such as drug use and sales and reference theft peaked in medium-sized cities.

Over 40% of respondents personally had been the victim of a crime in the library.

The lowest level of crime was found in libraries in Scotland.

Institutional and personal costs of crime were common in the libraries studied. There were significant expenses related to crime as well as changes in policy and individual behavior. English and Welsh libraries experienced greater costs than libraries in Scotland.

Approximately one quarter of the sample indicated that the impact of crime on services was "moderate" or "severe."

REFERENCES

Hoppe, Ronald and Simmel, Edward, "Book tearing and the bystander in the university library," *College and Research Libraries*, 30, (1969): 247-251.

Lincoln, Alan Jay, *Crime in the Library: A Study of Patterns, Impact and Security.* (New York: R.R. Bowker), 1984.

Lincoln, Alan Jay and Lincoln, Carol Z., "The impact of crime in public libraries," *Library and Archival Security*, 3, (1980):125-137.

United States Department of Justice, *Report to the Nation on Crime and Justice*, (Washington, D.C.), 1983.

Chapter Three

Library Crime in Canada

The second project of the library crime series focused on Canadian public libraries. Canada, the second largest country in the world, has the briefest national history of the countries examined. The first federalization of territories occurred in 1867, and continued until 1949, when the province of Newfoundland was added. While each province has its own government with autonomy in many spheres, the federal government is the central authority. The population is diverse in origin with strong British and French components. Other European, native, and Asian peoples also comprise significant groupings.

From the viewpoint of a criminologist there have been somewhat unusual historical developments in the patterns of crime. Whereas England and the United States had declining crime from the middle 1800s until after World War I, Canada has shown a general increase from the early days until modern times.

CRIME TRENDS

Even though crime in Canada has been rising over the past century it is still below that of the United States but somewhat higher than the rates in Great Britain. Canadian national crime statistics are broken down into three general categories: violent (homicide and attempted murder, sexual assault, robbery and assault); property (breaking and entering, motor vehicle theft, theft, fraud and possession of stolen goods); and other offenses (includes vandalism and drug offenses). Summaries of the major patterns of reported crimes are shown in Table 3.1. In 1983 there were nearly 2.2 million violent, property, and other offenses, for a rate of approximately 8,600 crimes per 100,000 population. If just violent and property crimes are included, then the total was 1.6 million offenses with a rate of

Table 3.1

Canadian Crime Rates (1983)

Type of Crime	Rate per 100,000	
Violent	686	
Homicide	2.7	
Rape	11	
Wounding and assault	511	(1982)
Robbery	97	
Property	5,703	
Breaking and entering	1,452	
Theft	3,371	
Motor vehicle theft	304	

about 6,500. Almost 95% of these were property crimes. The statistics on property crimes include possession of stolen goods and fraud, categories which are not included in the U.S. Index crimes. Theft is the most common of the property crimes. It comprises about 60% of that category. Breaking and entering comprises just over a quarter of property offenses. To provide some historical perspective, it should be noted that the rate of property crime has tripled in the last 20 years.

Violent crime also has increased dramatically in the last two decades, showing more than a threefold increase. However, there have been some recent declines in the murder rate. Assaults make up about 75%, and robberies about 16% of the violent crimes. Sexual assaults reflect less than 10%, while murder and attempted homicide comprise less than 1% of all violent crimes.

The crime data shown so far are based on the official reports of crime known to the police. Examination of statistics based on victimization surveys show higher levels for most crimes. The 1982 Canadian Urban Victimization Survey, conducted in seven major metropolitan areas, found that 71% of personal property thefts were not reported to police. Overall, more than half (59%) of the victimizations were not reported. Motor vehicle theft was the most likely to be reported. The same survey concluded that not reporting crime was associated with believing that the "offense was too minor" and that "police could do nothing about it." These reasons for failing to report crime are consistent with the major reasons that administrators of public institutions offer for choosing not to report crime in those settings.

City Size and Crime

The relationship between city size and the amount of crime is not a simple one. The overall pattern suggests that crime is higher in more densely populated areas than it is in others. But the relationship is far from perfect. For example, the five cities with the highest crime rates in 1982 all had a population of less than 75,000. In fact, Vancouver was the only major city among the 10 with the highest rates of crime. So while comparing categories of cities with increasing population does show increasing crime, there is also a great deal of variation within each of the population categories. (See Table 3.2.) Four of the seven major crimes (homicide, rape, robbery, and breaking and entering) show the highest rates in the largest cities. Theft was highest in cities of 50-100,000, while assault and motor vehicle theft peaked in cities of 100-250,000. Notice, however, that the assault rate was nearly as high in the smallest towns as well. Rape, robbery, breaking and entering, and motor vehicle theft did decline with each decline in city size. Other offenses such as gambling, vandalism and disorderly conduct actually had the highest rates in the smallest towns.

Provincial Differences

Canada, like any large and diverse nation, shows large regional fluctuations in crime patterns. There has been and continues to be a pattern of higher crime in the Western provinces and lower crime in the Maritime provinces. Overall, the North West and Yukon territories show the highest rates of crime. Quebec tends to be lower than average for total crimes, but among the highest for breaking and entering and robbery. British Columbia and Alberta have the highest rate of violent crime of the 10 provinces.

Offender Characteristics

Two factors, age and sex, were important in understanding patterns of offense in Great Britain. They also are important sources of variation in Canada's crime. when considering just juveniles, the peak age of property offense is the 12-15 year old group, while 16-17 year olds were more likely to appear for charges of violence. Compared with adults, juveniles had substantially higher rates of property crime and lower rates of violent crime. Among those clas-

Table 3.2
Canadian Crime Rates as a Function of Selected City Size (1977)

	\<2.5	5-10	25-50	50-100	100-250
Crime			City Size in 1,000s		
Homicide	1.7	1.3	1.9	1.6	3.2
Serious assault	493	376	448	362	501
Rape	4	4	7	8	9
Robbery	13	27	57	64	104
Breaking/entering	905	832	1,173	1,259	1,315
Theft	1,819	2,195	2,973	3,198	3,160
Auto theft	238	278	376	400	473

sified as adults, the young are disproportionately involved in crime. Adults between 20 and 24 are most likely to be imprisoned. Crime rates for both property and violent crimes peak relatively early and then decline rapidly.

Males are more likely to be involved in crime than females. This is true in all age categories. The greatest differences are for the crimes of violence. For example, in 1978 91% of charges for violent offenses involved males, while just over 80% of those charged with property offenses were males.

PROCEDURE FOR LIBRARY CRIME STUDY

The study of Canadian public libraries was carried out in three stages between late 1983 and early 1985, a period spanning 17 months. The total sample included every main and branch library with a complete address listed in Cattell's *American Library Directory*. A separate listing of Newfoundland's libraries was obtained and included in the sample. Altogether, nearly 1,400 librarians were sent the survey which contained 79 items along with a cover letter describing previous research and the current project. All recipients were assured that responses would be anonymous. An addressed, return envelope was included with each survey. A French translation was prepared for libraries in Quebec.

CHARACTERISTICS OF SAMPLE

Thirteen hundred and ninety surveys were distributed, and 477 completed returns were received prior to analysis. The return of 34% is within the average range for unsolicited surveys of this type. The size of this sample provides an opportunity to compare crime patterns along with variables of interest. The characteristics of the libraries and communities in which they are located will be described before turning to a description of the crime and disruption patterns in the libraries.

Institutional Factors

Number of patrons. The returns represent a full range of patron use. One fifth of the libraries served less than 20 patrons per day, and 25% served between 21 and 50. Approximately one fifth each reported 51-100, 101-250, and over 250 patrons on an average day.

Annual circulation. A second indicator of the activity level of the library is the annual circulation. For the analyses in this project the circulation was recorded only up to 99,000 per year. Exactly one third of the sample were recorded at that level. Some, of course, greatly exceeded 99,000. Twenty percent circulated 10,000 or fewer items, 20% circulated between 10,000 and 25,000, and 20% between 25,000 and 70,000.

Staff size. In each of the separate national studies the number of professional librarians, library aides/technicians, security staff and other staff was measured. The Canadian sample was dominated by libraries with one professional librarian (58%). An additional 21% had 2 or 3 librarians on the staff. Only 5% of the returns reported having 10 or more professional staff members. One quarter of the libraries had no aides, and were apparently a one-person operation. Thirty percent had 1 or 2 aides, and 15% had 10 or more aides. Only 10% of the sample employed security personnel, and most such libraries had one security employee. Other employees, usually custodians were on the staff of 45% of the libraries. The total number of employees averaged 12. Fifty-one percent had more than 5 staff members, and 31% more than 10. Large staffs (over 50) comprised on 4% of the sample.

City Size

The summary of Canadian crime statistics presented earlier in this chapter demonstrated that population level tends to be related to the rate of crime. When making comparisons between countries it also is important to be aware of the size of the cities being compared. Sixty percent of the returns from Canada were from cities or towns of less than 10,000. The largest category (32%) was from areas of less than 2,500 people. Just over a fifth of the surveys came from cities in excess of 50,000, with half of these from cities over 100,000. This sample represents population areas substantially smaller than those of the sample from Great Britain.

PATTERNS OF CRIME

The concerns raised in Chapter Two about legal definitions versus social definitions of crime apply to this study as well. Our concern again is with behavioral categories that provide as much information to administrators as possible. The same 24 crime and disruption items were assessed in Canada and Great Britain. Six of these were not included in the United States study conducted a year earlier. The general categories are vandalism/destruction, theft, problem patron behavior and assault.

Vandalism/Destruction

Intentional book damage. Book damage was reported by 65% of the libraries sampled. Sixteen percent reported 1 or 2 cases, and an additional 15% knew of 3-5 annual episodes. Over a fifth of the responses had over 10 repetitions. The average number of cases was 6.5 per year, or a rate of 650 cases per 100 libraries. Table 3.3 contains information on the proportion of libraries experiencing each of the crime items. Crime rates appear in Table 3.4.

> Our worst problem was a person who got severely drunk and urinate on $400 worth of books!

Vandalism inside. Slightly more than one third of the cases mentioned vandalism inside the building. Most of these libraries (20%) had 1 or 2 cases, but 7% had more than 6 occurrences. The rate (per 100 libraries) was 132.

Table 3.3

Proportion of Canadian Libraries Reporting Crime

Type of Episode	Number of Episodes					
	0	1-2	3-5	6-10	11-20	20+
Book damage	36	16	16	11	6	15
Vandalism outside	50	30	12	7	1	1
Vandalism inside	65	20	8	5	1	1
Equipment damage	89	7	2	2	1	0
Damage staff car	90	9	1	0	0	0
Damage patron car	94	5	1	0	1	0
Arson	96	4	0	0	0	0
Book theft	27	15	10	12	10	27
Reference theft	45	21	11	11	7	6
A V theft	89	6	2	1	0	1
Equipment theft	84	13	2	1	1	0
Fraudulent bill	91	8	0	1	0	0
Counterfeit money	98	2	0	0	0	0
Personal theft	77	18	3	1	1	0
Other theft	72	19	6	3	1	0
Forced entry	81	17	2	1	0	0
Drug use	90	7	1	1	1	1
Drug sales	96	3	0	1	0	0
Harassed patron	73	18	5	2	1	0
Harassed staff	57	20	11	5	4	3
Obscene calls	75	14	7	2	1	1
Indecent exposure	87	10	2	1	0	0
Assault on patron	95	4	1	0	0	0
Assault on staff	96	3	0	0	0	0
INDICES:						
Vandalism	22	19	14	12	14	19
Theft	21	14	11	8	12	34
Problem Patron	47	19	10	9	8	8
Assault	92	7	1	0	0	0
Total	12	10	12	10	10	46

We have never even had graffiti problems in the washrooms in the past seven years. The library is a vital part of the town's recreation.

Our public library is housed within the school library, therefore our problems are more peculiar to a school than a public library. Minor vandalism is the big issue.

Equipment damage. The rate of intentional equipment damage was low, 39/100. Only 11% of the sample had any problems. Four percent had 3 or more cases.

Vandalism outside. This problem was somewhat more common, occurring in exactly half of the libraries. Thirty percent had only 1

Table 3.4

Crime Rates in Canadian Libraries

Type of Episode	Rate per 100 libraries
Book damage	655
Vandalism outside	173
Vandalism inside	132
Equipment damage	39
Damage staff car	25
Damage patron car	18
Arson	5
Book theft	983
Reference theft	415
A V theft	53
Equipment theft	40
Fraudulent bill	16
Counterfeit money	9
Personal theft	57
Other theft	76
Forced entry	30
Drug use	39
Drug sales	11
Harassed patron	87
Harassed staff	251
Obscene calls	96
Indecent exposure	30
Assault on patron	10
Assault on staff	6
INDICES:	
Vandalism	1,036
Theft	1,642
Problem Patron	480
Assault	17
Total	2,996

or 2 episodes, but nearly 10% had 6 or more. The rate of vandalism outside the library was 173.

Vandalism to cars. Staff-owned cars were more likely to be reported vandalized than were patrons' cars. Only 6% of the sample told of a patron's car being damaged. Almost all of these cases were isolated incidents. Ten percent of the libraries knew of damage to a staff-owned car. Only 1% of the returns mentioned 6 or more acts of vandalism to staff cars. The rate of patron car damage (18/100) was slightly lower than that of staff car damage (25/100).

Arson. The most serious form of damage, arson, was relatively uncommon. One in 25 libraries experienced arson during the year. This means that 19 libraries in the sample actually reported arson. Sixteen of these had only one case, and 2 reported 2 cases. One library had between 3 and 5 repetitions. The estimated rate is 5/100.

Vandalism index. Over three quarters of the sampled libraries described an episode of vandalism. The average number of cases was 10 per year, or a rate of 1,030 per 100 libraries. Half of the sample had less than 5 acts of vandalism, and half had 5 or more. There were at least 25 cases in 15% of the libraries. Only 2% of the returns reported 50 or more cases of vandalism in or around the facility.

Theft

Books. The most common problems affecting the typical library is the theft of books. In this study, 73% of respondents were aware of some book theft. The most common response (27%) was that book theft occurred more than 20 times a year. An additional 10% reported between 10 and 20 episodes. Fifteen percent had only 1 or 2 cases, and 10% had 3-5. The average number of episodes of book theft (not the same as the number of books stolen) was 9.8, or a rate of 980. The overall pattern of book theft shows two distinct extremes. Approximately equal numbers of libraries reported no book theft as reported more than 20 cases.

> To our knowledge, no books were stolen, but some were checked out and never returned.
>
> It's hard to tell. Deliberate theft was assumed, but there can be many careless overdues.

Reference materials. Although not as common as the theft of books, reference theft was a chronic problem (over 6 times per year) in nearly 25% of the sample. More than half of the returns indicated that reference materials were stolen at least once, and over a third had 3 or more such thefts. The rate of reference theft was 415.

Audio-visual materials. Despite the obvious desirability of AV materials for thieves, the rate of theft was low. There were a reported 53 incidents per 100 libraries. It appears that accessibility to AV materials is more closely controlled than is access to books and reference material. Only 11% of respondents told of AV theft, and only 3% had 3 or more cases.

Book and nonbook resources. Thefts of books, reference materials and AV materials were examined in combination as an indicator of the theft of book and nonbook resources. No thefts were recorded in 25% of the sample. The second quarter of the sample reported between 1 and 7 thefts, while an additional quarter had between 8 and 25 incidents. The final quarter of the sample had over 25 cases. The average number of resource thefts was 14.5, a rate of 1450.

Equipment. Stealing equipment during operating hours is not easy to do without being detected. Thus, in many cases illegal entry to the library precedes equipment theft. Over 80% of the sampled libraries knew of no equipment theft. Thirteen percent had 1 or 2 thefts, and only 2% had chronic equipment theft. For every 100 libraries, there were an estimated 41 incidents involving theft of equipment.

Counterfeit money. Respondents in only 10 libraries (3%) reported that they were aware of counterfeit money's being passed in the library. All but one of these cases involved 1 or 2 incidents. How many cases went undetected is impossible to estimate.

Fraudulent billing. One in 10 of those responding said that they received at least one billing that was in some way fraudulent. In most cases this was an isolated event, but did occur 2 or more times in 4% of the sample.

Personal property. Among the favored targets of thieves in public settings are cash, credit cards and other personal items. Nearly a quarter (23%) of the surveys mentioned that personal property had been reported stolen. In about half of these cases it occurred only once. In 5% of the libraries there were 3 or more thefts of personal belongings. The rate of personal theft was 57/100.

> During the break-ins some personal property was stolen, i.e., knives, forks, a digital clock, a carpenter's tape.
>
> Up to 1983 there were a couple of thefts from the purses of staff which were left unattended and once from the overcoat pocket of the Chief Librarian.

Other theft. Theft of an item not specifically included in our questions occurred in 28% of the libraries. In nearly 20% of the sample, only 1 or 2 incidents were known. In 4% there were 6 or more repetitions. The rate was 78 incidents for each 100 libraries.

Breaking and entering. Close to one in five libraries experienced a break-in during the year. Almost all of these involved a single episode. The rate of break-ins was 30/100. In many cases it is clear that the illegal entry was tied to theft and vandalism.

In one 4 week period there were eight separate break-ins. The culprits were found and were discovered to be minors, i.e., 16 years of age or under. The "lawless ones" took money, stamps, calculators, three unlocked cash boxes; damaged the steel cabinet where the petty cash was kept; and poked into every nook, corner and filing cabinet in the library.

Theft index. The overwhelming majority (80%) of respondents reported at least 1 theft. Twenty percent had between 1 and 3 thefts, and another 20% experienced 4 to 15 thefts. Ten percent reported 45 or more separate incidents. The average annual number of thefts per library was 16.4, a rate of 1,643/100. Recall that the official rate of reported theft in Canada was about 3,375 per 100,000 individuals.

Problem Patron Behavior

The same definition of problem patron behavior is being used here as in Chapter 2. Behavior that is likely to be perceived as violating the norms of decent behavior for the library are included. Whether the behavior is illegal is not the major issue. Again, what is considered abusive or obscene is left to the discretion of the respondent, since it is either the respondent or a colleague who has to implement policies in the library and chooses how to react to problem patrons.

Drug use and sales. Drug use was detected more often than drug sales. Ten percent of the surveys mentioned drug use. In most cases it occurred only once or twice. Drug sales were reported by only 4% of the sample, and again tended to be a single episode. Even if drug use and sales are more widespread than our respondents indicated, they do not appear to be adversely affecting the libraries in our sample. The estimated rates of drug use and drug sales per 100 libraries were 38 and 11 respectively.

Verbal abuse. While not a physically threatening action by itself, verbal abuse may make people feel uncomfortable or unsafe. It is a direct assault upon the perception that the setting is one in which to work efficiently or relax and enjoy oneself. Patrons were verbally abused in 26% of the libraries. In two-thirds of these cases abusive incidents took place only once or twice. In 4% of the full sample there were 6 or more episodes of abuse. According to our respondents staff members were likely to be verbally abused than were patrons. More than 40% of the libraries in the sample had a staff member verbally abused. Unlike abuse to patrons, staff abuse tended to be repeated. Nine percent of the responses mentioned at least 6 cases of abuse of the staff. Rates were 86 for patron abuse and 250 for staff abuse.

> Our town has a population of about 400 with about 1,500 guys who work two weeks here and two weeks out. Every so often we have some mistreatment from one of them.
>
> Usually it's just the small children who like to argue, never the grown-ups.

Indecent exposure. More than 1 in 10 libraries (13%) reported acts of indecent exposure. In about half of these cases there was only one occurrence. Three or more cases were reported by 3% of the sampled libraries. The rate of indecent exposure was 30.

Obscene phone calls. One quarter of the returns reported that obscene phone calls were received by someone in the library. Most of these cases involved repeated incidents. For example, 6% had 2 occurrences, and 11% had 3 or more. An estimated 96 incidents occurred in each 100 libraries.

> I almost forgot to mention, for a period of two hears we have been bothered with obscene phone calls. However, we have received none in the past few months.

Problem patron index. Just over half of the libraries studied reported at least one problem with a patron. Twenty-five percent had fewer than 4 incidents, and 25% had between 4 and 23 episodes. Twenty-five or more separate problems occurred in 5% of the sample. The average number of problem patron events was 4.8 or 480 per 100 libraries.

Assault. The serious crime of assault against a patron occurred in only 6% of the sampled libraries. Of the 26 libraries reporting an assault, 19 of them had just one, 2 had 2 assaults, and 5 had 3 or more. The rate of assault on a patron was 10/100. Assault against a staff member was even less likely to occur. Returns from eighteen libraries (4%) mentioned an assault on an employee. Only five of these, 1% of the total, were repeated. The staff assault rate was 6/

100. Combining the two items shows that 8% of the sample had an assault in the library, with a rate of 17.

Personal Victimization

Approximately one out of every five people completing the survey was personally the victim of a crime while in the library. This question, unlike the others, asked about "ever" being a victim rather than victimization during the previous year. Single victimizations occurred in 14% of the cases, and respondents describing multiple crimes comprised 7% of the sample. What do we know about the people being victimized? Thirty-four percent of the 70 male employees and 19% of the 353 female employees who answered this question were victimized at some time in the library. Overall 7% were victims more than once. However, male respondents were more likely to experience multiple victimizations. Just over 20% reported two or more crimes against themselves, compared to only 5% of the female employees.

Total Crime

Almost 90% of the sample experienced some problem or crime that we asked about. Fifteen percent had three or fewer episodes. Half of the sample had more than 17 repetitions. The high crime libraries, the 10% with most problems, experienced over 80 different incidents. The low crime libraries reportedly were crime free. The average number of incidents approached 30. For every 100 libraries there were 2,996 crimes or disruptive episodes reported to us. As was true with the British sample, the sum of the indices does not equal the Total Index because cases with missing data (skipped a question) were not included in the Total. Recall that the national crime statistics for Canada reported about 8,600 criminal violations per 100,000 population. Even if all infractions of provincial and municipal ordinances are added to that total, there are only 11,000 offenses/100,000 people. This converts to 11 offenses per 100, dramatically lower than the institutional rate we have found. The opposite conversion, from 100 to 100,000 hypothetical libraries would result in a rate of nearly 3 million separate offenses. Of course, comparing institutions with individuals is not a fair comparison. Yet, the magnitude of the problem can be seen in a somewhat different perspective when these comparisons are made.

INSTITUTIONAL FACTORS RELATED TO CRIME

The analysis of the data from the study of Great Britain's libraries found that several characteristics of the institution were related to the amount and type of crime. The activity level of the library was one significant factor. This will be examined again for Canadian libraries, along with the potential relationships between the age of patrons and the likelihood of crime.

Number of patrons. Servicing large numbers of patrons is likely to increase the demand for resources. This increased demand may at times be met by inappropriate use of these "scarce" resources. The correlation between the number of patrons and the levels of the various crime items was significant except for assault on staff members. That is, as the average number of patrons increased, the level of the various crimes tended to increase. The strongest relationships were between patron activity level and crimes involving book resources. There was a strong correlation ($r. = .50$) between patron activity and book theft. Relationships that were nearly as strong were found for reference theft ($r. = .46$) and intentional book damage ($r. = 46$). Verbal abuse to staff ($r. = .35$) and vandalism inside the building ($r. = .31$) showed the next strongest associations. The full listing of correlations is shown in Table 3.5.

The number of patrons using the library also was positively correlated with each of the crime indices. The strongest association was with the combined theft index ($r. = .56$) and the weakest with assault ($r. = .11$).

Is there still a strong relationship with patron activity if the size of the city is controlled for? When partial correlations are computed to determine the association between the number of patrons and the level of crime within the separate categories of city size, the effect is still significant. Furthermore, as would be expected given the significant correlations, within cities of the same size, many of the crime rates increase as the number of patrons increases. Book theft, for example, in towns between 2,500 and 10,000 rises from an average of one episode per library when there were less than 10 patrons per day to over 11 episodes in libraries serving over 250 patrons daily. Similar book theft patterns were found as well in the libraries in cities of other sizes. However, not all crimes showed this pattern. The frequency of episodes with problem patrons was affected more by city size than by the level of patron activity. Several of the vandalism items increased along with the number of pa-

Table 3.5

Correlations of Crime Items with
Institutional Factors and City Size

Type of Episode	# Patrons	Circulation	City Size
Book damage	.46	.40	.47
Vandalism outside	.26	.24	.22
Vandalism inside	.31	.26	.30
Equipment damage	.21	.17	.22
Damage staff car	.16	.12	.17
Damage patron car	.13	.07	.10
Arson	.12	.14	.19
Book theft	.50	.43	.52
Reference theft	.46	.44	.45
A V theft	.13	.07	.14
Equipment theft	.15	.15	.19
Fraudulent bill	.08	.09	.02
Counterfeit money	.08	.06	.13
Personal theft	.24	.21	.24
Other theft	.21	.14	.18
Forced entry	.18	.08	.10
Drug use	.13	.12	.19
Drug sales	.08	.05	.09
Harassed patron	.21	.20	.25
Harassed staff	.35	.32	.43
Obscene calls	.26	.15	.35
Indecent exposure	.21	.19	.20
Assault on patron	.12	.12	.14
Assault on staff	.04	-.02	.01
INDICES:			
Vandalism	.51	.42	.50
Theft	.57	.46	.58
Problem Patron	.42	.34	.52
Assault	.11	.07	.10
Total	.61	.47	.64

r=.08 (p<.05)
r=.11 (p<.01)
r=.13 (p<.001)

trons, but only in the smaller cities and towns. To illustrate, the vandalism index for libraries in cities of 10-50,000 rose from 6 episodes per library with less than 20 patrons per day to 23 in libraries reporting over 250 patrons on an average day. Yet in the largest cities the number of patrons did not affect the vandalism rate (51-100 patron = 19; over 250 patron = 17).

Patron age. Canada, like other countries, exhibits a pattern of higher crime by and against the young. Would there be similar patterns in the library? To pursue this question respondents were asked to estimate the proportion of patrons between the ages of 12-18, 19-55, and over 55. The first group typifies the high-risk age group. Serving higher proportions of young people may increase the likelihood of certain types of crime and disruption in the library. However, the correlations between the proportion of 12-18 year olds and the crime items generally were not significant. The exception was the level of drug sales in the library. This relatively uncommon crime was more common in libraries with many 12-18 year olds. None of the other crime items was associated with increasing proportions of youth.

> We have good relations with the school children and the people of this community. We haven't had any problems to speak of.

Annual circulation. To what extent does the level of circulation relate to the level of crime? The strongest associations were with reference theft ($r. = .44$), book theft ($r. = .43$) and intentional book damage ($r. = .40$). In addition, most of the other crime items were correlated with circulation level. Several, however, were not. These included drug sales, vandalism to patron's cars and assault on staff. Each of the crime indices, except assault, was correlated with the level of circulation. The strongest association was with the theft index, followed by vandalism and problem patron behavior. The level of crime occurring outside the library was not as strongly associated with the number of patrons as was the level of crime occurring inside the building.

Staff size. The size of the professional staff was related to several of the crime items, but not as strongly as were patron activity and circulation. The strongest of these associations were with the theft of equipment ($r. = .21$) and vandalism inside the library ($r. = .17$). Other positive correlations were found, including book damage, reference theft, vandalism to equipment, and drug sales. Examination of the indices showed that vandalism was most strongly associated. The size of the nonprofessional staff showed a stronger relationship to the amount of crime. All of the crime items, except assaults, tended to increase along with the size of the nonprofessional staff.

COMMUNITY FACTORS

The importance of city size was demonstrated by the analysis of the data from Great Britain. Once again we will show that crime in libraries varies along with population. Several other community factors were also examined as part of the Canadian study. Estimates of the social class of the neighborhood surrounding the library as well as descriptions of the typical types of neighborhood housing were obtained. We also asked about the location of various community facilities and agencies in relation to the library. That is, the proximity of the library to schools, police stations, and parks was examined as a possible factor related to crime patterns show similar differences. We will examine this possibility first.

Provincial Differences

The study was designed to allow for comparisons of the crime rates between libraries in each of the provinces and territories. For the most part this can be done. Adequate returns were obtained from all areas except Prince Edward Island and the Yukon Territory. Both of these had fewer than 10 returns. The largest number of returns came from Ontario, Quebec, and British Columbia. This is consistent with the distribution of libraries in Canada. The breakdown of the returns by province is shown in Table 3.6 along with the respective crime rates.

Judging by national Canadian crime patterns, we would expect to find higher levels of library crime in the western provinces and territories. While this overall pattern was found, it did not hold for all different types of crime and disruption. Some of the discrepancies can be accounted for by differences in the average city size of the libraries. Libraries from Ontario, Quebec and British Columbia were more likely to be found in larger cities, a condition that would contribute to higher levels of crime. Several provincial comparisons, controlling for city size, will be made to illustrate this proposition. In all cases the reported figures represent the rate of crime per 100 libraries.

> We are a little unusual in that we are in the Arctic, where we don't have typical southern notions of day and night. We have 24-hour sunlight for 2-3 months and then 24-hour darkness for a couple of months in the winter. Problems connected with this seem to have more to do with the seasons than the amount of daylight . . . when it starts to get cold and the days get short, the prospect of another eight-month-long winter of -30 to -40 degrees C. seems to inspire people to heave rocks through the library windows.

Table 3.6

Crime Rates/100 by Province

Type of Episode	NF	NS	NB	QC	ON	MB	SK	AB	BC	NWT
Book damage	178	563	413	863	757	615	600	600	732	270
Vandalism outside	90	95	194	200	172	176	136	147	271	120
Vandalism inside	43	40	31	174	153	127	218	113	108	340
Equipment damage	2	67	0	56	43	52	27	19	36	40
Damage staff car	0	124	12	23	18	6	45	6	54	0
Damage patron car	0	0	0	25	27	6	0	6	19	10
Arson	0	0	0	8	5	21	9	0	2	10
Book theft	275	763	693	1031	1071	851	1200	1176	1389	922
Reference theft	140	314	175	322	489	197	544	459	672	544
A V theft	9	250	13	*	50	15	273	15	27	44
Equipment theft	10	40	25	63	45	3	40	13	60	10
Fraudulent bill	0	10	19	*	20	15	9	15	4	89
Counterfeit money	0	0	6	*	17	0	0	21	2	0
Personal theft	39	45	13	*	51	45	191	15	100	33
Other theft	50	42	67	47	79	88	182	76	102	80
Forced entry	30	15	19	*	31	21	45	43	36	33
Drug use	0	38	127	22	21	3	381	75	65	40
Drug sales	0	124	0	5	5	6	0	6	10	10
Harassed patron	43	62	38	67	95	48	230	106	131	100
Harassed staff	28	162	125	293	298	264	391	100	319	150
Obscene calls	0	88	119	*	138	56	45	8	95	0
Indecent exposure	0	43	13	62	29	15	45	6	32	50
Assault on patron	0	5	0	30	9	3	45	0	7	0
Assault on staff	2	0	13	25	6	0	0	0	0	0
INDICES:										
Vandalism	315	867	640	1356	1169	1003	760	894	1210	790
Theft	386	1694	1007	*	1741	1236	2400	1425	2456	1887
Problem Patron	58	618	427	*	554	403	467	164	655	333
Assault	2	5	13	54	15	3	45	0	7	0
Total	761	3184	2087	*	3479	2645	3672	2483	4328	3010

* (not measured/missing items)

Vandalism. The rate of intentional book damage was highest in Quebec (864) and Ontario (757), followed closely by British Columbia (732) and Manitoba (615). The lowest rate was found in Newfoundland (178) (see Table 3.5). However, city size played a role in these patterns. Quebec had higher rates in smaller cities (700) than did British Columbia (245), but in the larger cities the rates in British Columbia (1750) were substantially higher than in Quebec (850). Vandalism outside the building peaked in British Columbia (270), followed by Quebec (200) and New Brunswick (194). Low rates were recorded in Newfoundland and Nova Scotia (95). Vandalism inside the library was high in N.W.T. (340), Saskatchewan (218) and Quebec (174). The least serious problems were recorded in New Brunswick (31) and Newfoundland (43).

Vandalism to patrons' cars parked around the library was most common in Ontario (27) and Quebec (25), and not reported at all in several other provinces. Nova Scotia (124) had the peak rate of vandalism to staff-owned cars, followed by British Columbia (54) and Saskatchewan (45). No incidents were reported in Newfoundland and NWT. Damage to equipment was above average in Nova Scotia (67) and Quebec (56), but low in New Brunswick and Newfoundland. The rate of arson was highest in Manitoba (21), and not reported at all in several areas. Overall, the highest reported rate of vandalism was found in Quebec (1356) and British Columbia (1211), followed by Ontario (1169) and Manitoba (1003). The lowest overall rates were reported by libraries in Newfoundland (315) and New Brunswick (640).

Theft. Book theft rates followed the national trends of higher rates in the western provinces. British Columbia (1389) had the top rate, followed by Saskatchewan (1200) and Alberta (1176). Quebec and Ontario also had slightly higher than average rates. Unusually low rates were recorded in Newfoundland (275). Within most of the provinces book theft rates tended to increase as the size of the city increased. For example, towns under 10,000 in British Columbia reported rates of about 800, while cities over 100,000 had book theft rates of over 2300. Similarly, in the low theft province of Newfoundland, the small towns reported theft rates of 57, which increased to 1200 in cities of 10-50,000.

Reference theft rates were high in British Columbia (672), NWT (544) and Ontario (489). Newfoundland (140) and New Brunswick (175) had the lowest rates. Equipment theft peaked in Quebec (627) and British Columbia (603), while Manitoba (3) and NWT (10) were low. The western province libraries indicated more problems with other thefts (Saskatchewan, 182; British Columbia, 102; Manitoba, 88). Similarly, breaking and entering occurred at stronger rates in the west. Saskatchewan (45) and Alberta (43) had the highest levels. The lowest rates were found in Nova Scotia (15) and New Brunswick (19). Reports of passing counterfeit money came primarily from Alberta and Ontario. Fraudulent billing was at its highest level in NWT (89), and was substantially lower in all other provinces.

Personal property theft was particularly high in Saskatchewan (191) and British Columbia (100), while New Brunswick (13) and Alberta (15) reported the lowest rates. Audio visual materials thefts showed wide discrepancies. Saskatchewan (273) and Nova Scotia

(250) rates were far above the rates of the next province, Ontario (50).

Two separate theft indices were computed. Materials thefts was most prominent in British Columbia (2125), Saskatchewan (2022) and NWT (1650), and least problematic in Newfoundland (321) and New Brunswick (880). The total theft index showed identical patterns. Rates ranged from 2455 in British Columbia to 386 in Newfoundland.

Problem patron behavior. Reports of drug use ranged widely. Saskatchewan libraries had a rate of 382, substantially above the next highest rate, which occurred in New Brunswick (127). Newfoundland and Manitoba libraries reported no problems. In contrast, drug sales in the library were highest in Nova Scotia (124), followed by British Columbia (10). The unusually high rates in Nova Scotia can be accounted for by two major libraries with chronic problems. Verbal abuse of other patrons was most problematic in the western provinces and lowest in New Brunswick. Verbal abuse of the staff ranged from Saskatchewan (391), British Columbia (319) and Quebec (293) to Newfoundland (27).

Incidents of indecent exposure were most common in Quebec (62) and NWT (50), while low rates were recorded in Alberta (5), New Brunswick (13) and Manitoba (15). Finally, obscene phone calls to the library peaked in Ontario (138) and New Brunswick (119). Libraries in several provinces reported no incidents. British Columbia's libraries had the highest overall rate of problem patron behavior (656), closely followed by those in Nova Scotia (618) and Ontario (554). Low rates were recorded in Newfoundland (58) and Alberta (164).

Assault. As shown earlier, assaults in the library are uncommon. The highest rates of assault on a patron were found in Saskatchewan (45) and Quebec (30). Several provinces were free of attacks on patrons. Staff assaults were at their highest in Quebec (25). Quebec's libraries also had the highest total assault rate (55), followed by Saskatchewan (45) and Ontario (15).

Total crime. The highest overall rate of library crime and disruption appeared in British Columbia's libraries (4,328), followed by those in Saskatchewan (3,672) and Ontario (3,479). The lowest overall rate was in Newfoundland (761). It should be noted that, as a result of an error, several of the crime items were omitted from the translated version of the survey used in Quebec. This made it impossible to compute several of the indices. However, when comparing the 18 crime items that were included, the rates of crime in Quebec were among the highest of those in all the provinces.

City Size

The relationship between city size and the amount of crime in the library is strong. All correlations except for assault against staff show that as the population of the area increases the amount of crime in the library increases. This is not surprising. Recall that the general crime statistics for Canada showed that the assault rate was almost as high in small towns as in major cities. The positive correlations show that a general relationship of change in the same direction is occurring. This does not mean that there is an increase in crime for every single increase in population, but a similar overall pattern of change is emerging. In some cases, increases in crime in cities of a certain size may appear and then be followed by a stabilization or decline in crime. The strongest associations with population were for the level of book theft ($r. = .52$), book damage ($r. = .47$), reference theft ($r. = .45$), abuse to staff ($r. = .43$) and vandalism inside the library ($r. = .30$). The weakest significant correlations were for drug sales, assault on patron, passing counterfeit money and vandalism to patrons' cars.

> This is a quite small town with a very low crime rate. We just don't have any problems in the library.
>
> No problems—The quiet life in O_____ appears to have its advantages.

The comparisons between the actual rates of crime in each category of city size are informative. Some types of crime (e.g., book theft) show a constant increase as city size increases from under 2,300 to over 500,000. The average number of separate book theft episodes in the smallest cities' libraries was 3.5. This increased to 8.6 in cities between 2,500 and 10,000; to 14.0 in cities of 10-50,000; 17.4 in cities of 50-100,000; 18.5 in cities of 100-500,000; and 18.8 in cities of over 500,000 people. However, this pattern was not typical of all the crime items. About half, including book damage, drug use and sales, vandalism to cars and inside the building, and verbal abuse peaked in cities between 100-500,000, and dropped in the largest cities (see Table 3.7).

Table 3.7

Crime Rates as a Function of City Size

Type of Episode	City Size in 1,000s					
	<2.5	2.5-10	10-50	50-100	100-500	+500
Book damage	222	461	840	1,449	1,500	1,123
Vandalism outside	73	133	318	262	287	173
Vandalism inside	28	82	213	279	353	162
Equipment damage	8	12	50	116	105	114
Damage staff car	5	6	28	64	121	32
Damage patron car	5	4	39	35	58	4
Arson	0	4	3	14	8	32
Book theft	345	856	1,401	1,737	1,847	1,878
Reference theft	59	265	609	1,239	900	748
A V theft	19	33	52	141	200	40
Equipment theft	14	17	67	103	127	24
Fraudulent bill	9	20	22	38	7	0
Counterfeit money	1	4	2	7	3	130
Personal theft	14	13	115	152	160	75
Other theft	36	71	107	118	150	78
Forced entry	15	26	56	52	39	19
Drug use	4	21	44	38	171	127
Drug sales	3	3	3	2	92	18
Harassed patron	22	77	106	119	235	205
Harassed staff	52	108	343	503	808	686
Obscene calls	21	46	75	204	431	224
Indecent exposure	11	11	26	121	84	39
Assault on patron	4	2	20	10	24	27
Assault on staff	6	6	6	10	2	14
INDICES:						
Vandalism	341	698	1,531	2,282	2,432	1,586
Theft	498	1,248	2,569	3,773	3,861	2,756
Problem Patron	107	266	649	932	1,614	1,353
Assault	10	8	26	21	26	41
Total	863	2,145	4,790	6,870	8,238	5,679

Several other crime rates peaked in cities of 50-100,000 and dropped in the larger cities. These included reference theft, vandalism outside and to equipment, breaking and entering, indecent exposure and fraudulent billing. For example, the average number of reference thefts in the smallest town libraries was .6 but increased to 2.6 in communities of 2,500-10,000 and 6.1 in cities of 10-50,000. Reference theft peaked in cities between 50-100,000 at 12.4 per library and then declined to 9.0 in cities of 100-500,000 and 7.5 in the largest cities. Several possibilities may explain this type of pattern. It may be that more episodes go undetected in the larger libraries. It is also possible that there is increased security in large city libraries, and this serves to keep some crime under control. Finally, there are more branches in the larger cities, that is, many returns from the larger cities actually are from small libraries with relatively low circulation and patron activity. Does a relatively small library in a big city show crime patterns similar to other small libraries or to other urban libraries? These possibilities can be examined by looking at the relationship between the combined factors of city size and activity levels.

When libraries in the largest cities are compared according to their patron activity levels, we find some evidence to support the last hypothesis. For example, the average level of book damage in the large city (over 500,000) libraries serving fewer than 250 patrons per day was only 7.2 while in the libraries serving more than 250 patrons it rose to 14.6. Similarly, book theft was lower in the less active libraries (16.2) than in the busiest libraries (21.1). The same comparison shows that reference thefts in the largest cities varied from an average of 3.4 to 11.4.

Social Class of Neighborhood

Each recipient was asked to describe the social class of the neighborhood in which the library was located. The majority (66%) indicated that the library was in a "middle class" (MC) area. Nearly a fifth (19%) of the areas were described as "lower middle class" (LMC), and 11% were labeled "upper middle class" (UMC). Approximately 2% each were described as lower or upper class areas. Does the social class of the neighborhood relate to the level of crime? Overall, the answer is yes. Examination of the Total Index shows that LMC libraries had the highest crime rate (4,136), followed by MC libraries (2,768) and UMC libraries (2,456). Not all of the crime indices showed these systematic changes as a function of social class. Theft, problem patron behavior and assault were higher in less affluent locations. Vandalism rates peaked in LMC (1,359), followed by UMC libraries (1,152) and were lowest in MC settings (936).

> Social class of the neighborhood? We are in the downtown business district, one street about two blocks long. I find it hard to define the "social classes" up here, as it is a different kind of society. The population mix consists of a large number of southerners, who are a transient population. . . Native Indians and Eskimos comprise the other 2/3 of the population, and are engaged in all sorts of occupations. . . . This mix doesn't lend itself to the kind of social class definitions you are probably used to.

Many of the individual crime items showed substantial decreases as the economic level of the neighborhood increased. For example, book theft dropped from a rate of 1,245 (LMC) to 907 (MC) and 750 (UMC). Similarly, the theft of personal property was highest in LMC libraries (113), dropping to moderate levels in MC locations (50) and showing still further reductions in the UMC libraries (24). There also were large differences in the reported rates of verbal abuse to staff members. The highest levels were recorded in LMC libraries (369), followed by MC (242) and UMC libraries (191). Drug use was dramatically higher in LMC libraries (61) than in MC (31) or UMC libraries (2).

Several crime items were not related to neighborhood social class. These included book damage, reference theft, vandalism outside the building (highest in UMC libraries), damage to patrons' cars, arson, breaking and entering (which increased as social class increased), passing counterfeit money and fraudulent billing.

Proximity of Schools

It would be reasonable to hypothesize that being closer to schools might raise the level of those crimes typically committed by the young. However, the overall trends were not strong. Only vandalism, particularly outside the building, and assault were higher when the library was close to schools. Most theft and problem patron items were not closely related to school proximity, or if they were the effects involved combinations of factors that we did not examine.

> The library is a school-public library. We work with the kids all the time. The worst things that we see are some damage and some rough-housing.

COSTS OF CRIME

The effect of crime on the library will be examined first at the institutional level. This includes responses such as closing, changing schedules and expenditures related o crime. Then we will turn to material related to the personal costs of crime such as avoiding work, using escorts, and carrying protective devices.

Institutional Costs

Financial losses. One of the most direct ways to measure the cost of crime in the library is to assess the actual dollar losses resulting from crime during the year. Under one fifth of the sample reported no losses due to crime during the previous 12 months (see Table 3.8). An additional 18% had less than $100 (Canadian) in losses. Over 25% indicated that their losses were between $250 and $1,000. One in 20 libraries had losses between $5,000 and $10,000, while 2% suffered losses exceeding $10,000. The highest loss levels were in British Columbia and Quebec. The lowest average losses were in Newfoundland. The amount of loss was positively correlated with increasing city size (r. = .49), patron activity levels (r. = .50), and circulation level (r. = .38). Among the individual crime items the strongest relationships were with the problems of book theft, reference theft, and book damage.

> I have no record of the money involved, as we are a branch of a library system, and such problems are handled for the system as a whole by HQ.

Table 3.8

Crime Losses and Prevention Costs

Dollars Lost	% Reporting
None	19
<100	18
101-250	17
251-500	14
501-1,000	14
1,001-2,500	8
2,501-5,000	4
5,000-10,000	5
>10,000	2
Crime Prevention Expenses	
None	74
<$250	13
251-500	4
501,1,000	2
1,001-2,500	3
2,501-5,000	1
5,001-10,000	1
>10,000	2

Crime prevention expenses. In addition to the actual losses resulting from past crimes, there may be costs related to preventing subsequent crimes. Respondents were asked to report their crime prevention expenses. Nearly three quarters (74%) of the libraries had no crime prevention expenditures for the year. Thirteen percent more spent less than $250, and an additional 6% less than $1,000. Only 3% spent over $5,000. Libraries in Quebec and Saskatchewan had the highest average crime prevention expenses; the Northwest Territories, Alberta and Newfoundland had the lowest. Libraries in larger cities, with higher circulation and more patrons, were likely to spend more on crime prevention. Several crime items were good indicators of the likelihood of spending for crime prevention. These included verbal abuse to staff, indecent exposure, reference theft and vandalism inside the building. It is interesting that the decision to deploy security is more closely associated with "offensive" behavior than with theft. A full description of security patterns can be found in Chapter 5.

Total expenses. Combined expenses of crime losses and crime prevention are an indicator of the total financial costs of crime. Approximately 10% of the sample had total crime expenses in excess of $10,000. Only 1% reportedly had combined losses and prevention costs of over $20,000. Quebec and British Columbia had the highest total expenses, while Newfoundland and Alberta reported the lowest crime related expenses. Just over 15% of the sample reported neither losses nor crime prevention expenses.

Closed the library. How often did crime cause such widespread damage that the library was forced to close or decisions were made to close voluntarily? Of the approximately 500 libraries for which data are available, only 10 (2%) closed during the year. Surprisingly, data indicate that libraries in Newfoundland were the most likely to close. Only one facility was closed more than once. What was related to a library closing? the best indicators were the level of theft, breaking and entering, indecent exposure and arson. In one case we receive a survey about six months later than most. The respondent offered apologies and indicated that the library had been badly damaged by fire and forced to close. Given the few cases in which a facility closed, these trends should be viewed with care. Reports of a branch library's being closed were similar.

Changing hours. A less drastic response to crime is to alter the operating schedule. For example, if high levels of crime inside the library tend to occur on Friday or Saturday evening, then reducing hours on those evenings may alleviate the problem. Of course, maintaining the hours and taking other security precautions might be a preferred response. Only 2% of the surveys included reports of a changed schedule, half of these once and half many times. Libraries in smaller communities were more likely to change their schedule. Only one library in a community with population over 10,000 did so.

Inoperable equipment. Vandalism and theft may result in the loss or use of equipment. This occurred in 30 libraries (7%) during the year. In one third of the cases this occurred more than once. Since over 75 libraries reported that equipment actually had been stolen, it appears that most libraries do replace their lost equipment, with resulting impact on the operating budget. Problems of this sort were associated primarily with larger cities and higher levels of patron activity. Nova Scotia's and British Columbia's libraries had peak rates of lost equipment.

Discontinued programs. Occasionally there may be programs run by the public library that turn out to be too risky in terms of increased crime. This can occur for several reasons. In some cases, the program may bring potential offenders into the building. Alternately, the program may attract a group that becomes targets of either protest activity or crime. In either case the program may be discontinued. This occurred in 5% of the responding libraries, about half of these more than once. There were major provincial differences. over a third of the libraries in Nova Scotia reported that programs had been stopped. The crimes most closely associated with decisions to stop programs were the sale of drugs and theft of equipment. City size, circulation level and number of patrons were not related to cancelling community programs.

Calling police. The initial response to some problems in public institutions is to call police. Typically this is most likely to occur when there are injuries or threats of injury, large thefts or widespread destruction. Over 40% of the sample called police to the library at least once. Nearly 10% called police 6 or more times during the year. What factors are associated with calling the police? Again, the more active libraries were more likely to call. Institutions in cities over 10,000 were equally likely to call police, but police were less likely to be called in the smaller communities. Vandalism inside the building and to equipment, theft of personal property as well as breaking and entering were the problems most closely associated with calling police. This response was most common in Quebec, Northwest Territories and British Columbia. The lowest average number of police requests was by libraries in Newfoundland.

Institutional impact. A summary measure of reactions to crime was computed using the non-financial items above. Nearly half (45%) of the sample reported at least one of the institutional responses to crime. Twenty-six percent had multiple responses. The highest overall impact was found in Nova Scotia, British Columbia and Quebec.

Effect on services. Decisions to close, change schedule, losing equipment, and so on may produce an impact on services to the public. Respondents were asked to estimate how much crime and disruption affect their service to the public. Almost half (47%) said that there was no effect on services, while 38% indicated that service was affected very little. The remaining 15% reported that crime affected the library moderately or a great deal. Perceived impact peaked in cities between 50-100,000 and then dropped in the largest cities. Reports from Quebec indicated the highest level of perceived impact. Low levels were found in Newfoundland and Saskatchewan. The strongest associations were with the theft of equipment (r. = .28), intentional book damage (r. = .24) and abuse to staff (r. = .23). Notice that these are not all among the most serious crimes that occur in the library but are the ones that affect day to day functioning. The perceived effect also was strongly associated with calling the police (r. = .25).

Personal Costs

Along with institutional effects, staff may be affected by crime as well. Behavioral responses by staff range from carrying protective devices to being picked up after work. Only one respondent indicated that he or she carried any protective device while at work, and less than 1% knew of a staff member that did. However, 10% of the respondents did not answer the question. It may be premature to suggest that staff do not carry any protective devices. There were other behavioral reactions to crime. A small group of employees (3%) indicated that they tried to avoid working after dark. This response was associated with the rate of assault (r. = .30) and indecent exposure (r. = .26) in the library. Similarly, 4% of respondents mentioned that staff asked not to work after dark. Assault rates were related to these requests as well (r. = .39). Higher proportions (19%) indicated that they were picked up after work and were escorted to their cars as a crime prevention measure. Being picked up also was more common when there were high levels of assault and indecent exposure. Escort policies were associated with most of the major crime categories; but particularly with verbal abuse of the staff and the rate of obscene phone calls. Staff training sessions to handle crime and disruption problems were conducted in 13% of the libraries. It was most closely linked to the rate of verbal abuse, book theft and obscene phone calls. City size also was related to the more common personal responses. Being picked up after work and escorted to cars were more common in the larger cities. For example, with no one in towns under 2,500 was escorted to his or her car, over 25% of respondents in cities of at least 50,000 were escorted. Libraries in New Brunswick and Quebec showed the highest overall personal costs. (See Table 3.9)

SUMMARY

Even though Canadian crime has been rising over the past century it is still below the rates in the U.S., but somewhat higher than the rates in Great Britain.

Book theft, the most common crime, was reported by nearly 75% of the sample. The rate of book theft was 983/100. Book damage

Table 3.9
Personal and Institutional Effects of Crime

Institutional Impact:	Rate per 100 Libraries
Closed library	3
Closed branch library	2
Changed operating hours	3
Lost use of equipment	11
Stopped community programs	10
Called police	90
Training session	14

Staff Impact:	Proportion Reporting
Avoid work after dark	3%
Picked up after work	10%
Escorted to car	10%

also was common, noted by two thirds of the sample. The rate of book damage was 655/100.

High crime libraries, (in the top 10%) each reported more than 80 separate episodes of crime and disruption.

The level of patron activity was closely related to thefts of library materials.

The number of the crimes increased as the size of the city in which the library was located increased.

There were major variations in crime from one province to another. The highest rates were in British Columbia and Saskatchewan.

Library crime was higher in lower middle-class areas than in middle-class and upper middle-class neighborhoods.

Nearly half of the libraries studied reported that there had been official institutional response, such as discontinuing programs or calling police, to the problem of crime.

Only 15% of the sample indicated that library services were moderately or strongly affected by crime.

Chapter Four

Three Studies of Library Crime

Many Americans consider crime to be among the major problems facing the nation. Opinion polls conducted over the last two decades have shown that concern about crime is often as great as concern about war, unemployment, disease, and medical care (Gallup, 1979, 1981). Furthermore, the majority of Americans report that they take some preventive action against being victimized when going out in public (Figgie, 1980). What is there about crime patterns in the United States that has led to this high level of concern? Are these crime patterns very different from those found in other places? We will consider these questions before we turn to a comparison of library crime patterns found in the United States with those found in Canada and Great Britain.

The major source of information about reported crime is the Uniform Crime Reports (UCR). Each year information on crimes reported to thousands of local police agencies is collected and analyzed. Data from the local agencies are tabulated for each state and then summarized regionally and nationally. The UCR have been published continuously since 1933 and provide an excellent way of making both temporal and state level comparisons of officially known crime. Crimes are divided into two major categories. Type One offenses include the most serious crimes: murder, rape, robbery, aggravated assault, burglary, larceny-theft and motor vehicle theft. Arson was added to this category in 1978. These major crimes comprise the Crime Index, a summary statistic of major crime in the United States. Violent and property crimes are the two obvious categories of the index. Type Two offenses include less serious offenses such as fraud, minor assaults, drug offenses, prostitution, vandalism and so on.

Violent Crime

The most common violent crime in the United States is aggravated assault. In 1982 there were over 650,000 incidents known to police. This is a rate of 281 per 100,000. As can be seen in Table 4.1 the rate of robbery was close behind at 232. Murder (9.1) and forcible rape (33.6) were substantially less common. The overall violent crime rate was 555.

Violent crime increased dramatically between 1960 and 1980. The rate of these crimes jumped from 161 in 1960 to over 575 in 1980. Rates of rape and robbery showed the greatest increases. In the last few years there has been a slight decline in some violent crimes. For example, the murder rate was 9.1 in 1982, but dropped to 8.3 in 1983 and 7.9 in 1984. While this is a welcome trend, the statistics are still depressing. In 1984, 18,700 people were murdered in the United States. The reported rate of rape rose 7% between 1983 and 1984, and aggravated assaults rose 5% in the same period. That same year over a million violent offenses were reported to police. Compared with Canada and Great Britain, violent crime rates in the United States are high. In contrast to the 1982 U.S. murder rate of 9.1, Canada reported a rate of 2.7, while Great Britain's rate was only 1.1. Reported rapes also are higher in the United States.

Property Crime

The vast majority, about 90%, of reported major crimes are property crimes. In 1982, the rate of property crime was just under 5,000, including over 3,000 larceny thefts and 1,475 burglaries. Similar to the changes in the patterns of violent crime, property crimes increased substantially between 1960 and 1980. The 1960 rate was just over 1,700, but rose to more than 5,300 in 1980. Once again there is evidence of recent declines. For example, between 1983 and 1984 there was a decline of 2% in the overall property crime rate. Since 1980 there has been a decline of over 10% in the index of the major violent and property crimes.

Cross-cultural comparisons of property crime are more difficult to make than are comparisons of violent crime. Differing definitions and categories complicate the task. However, some comparisons can be made. For example, the motor vehicle theft rate in the United States is approximately 500, while the Canadian rate is about 400.

Table 4.1

Crime Rates in the United States (1982)

Type of Crime	Rate per 100,000
Violent	555
Homicide	9
Rape	34
Aggravated assault	281
Robbery	232
Property	4,998
Burglary	1,475
Larceny-theft	3,070
Motor vehicle theft	453
Total	5,553

Larceny-theft rates are comparable. In 1980 the U.S. rate was 3156 and the Canadian rate was 3195. The rates in Great Britain were lower, with the theft rate just under 3,000.

Victimization Surveys

The second major source of data on crime patterns is the surveys of victims and potential victims of crime. While the statistics of officially reported crime are useful for making comparisons across locations and time they tend to be conservative estimates of the total amount of crime. Studies of victims of crimes have shown that many offenses go unreported. Reliable victim surveys of a cross section of the population have been conducted in the United States for more than a decade. These have shown a substantially higher rate of crime than is reported in the UCR. It is not uncommon for these victimization rates of violent crimes to be 2-3 times higher than the corresponding rates of officially known offenses. For example, the 1981 victimization rates of rape were 95, while the UCR rate was only 36. Similarly, the rates of robbery were higher in the victim surveys (741 vs. 251), while the rates of larceny were 3-4 times higher.

City Size and Crime

A striking feature of U.S. crime patterns is the variation that occurs as a function of city size. As was true of Canadian cities, the relationship between crime and city size is not a simple one. On the one hand, larger cities generally have higher total crime rates. On the other, examination of the separate crimes shows some breaks in this pattern. The crime index rate (major crimes) for 1983 was 5,159. This ranged from 1,990 in rural areas to 4,180 in cities under 10,000, and continued in an upward direction. Cities of 25-50,000 reported rates of 5,534; cities of 50-100,000 had rates of 5,999; while cities over 250,000 peaked at 8,639. Rape, robbery, aggravated assault, burglary and motor vehicle theft showed a continuous rise in rates as population increased. Murder rates were highest in cities over 250,000 (20.2) and next highest in cities between 100-250,000 (10.1). However, murder rates in rural areas (5.8) were higher than any city category up to 50,000. For example, cities below 10,000 had a murder rate of only 3.6. It should be pointed out that even at the low point murder rates are still higher than the national rates in either Canada or England. The other major inconsistency is for the larceny-theft rate, which peaked in cities between 100-250,000.

A more detailed look at serious crimes in some of the major U.S. cities points out the complexity of the relationship between city size and crime. In 1979 the highest murder rate was in Houston, a city with the eleventh greatest population. Burglary was highest in Las Vegas, Nevada, a city not even in the top 25 of population. Robbery rates, however, did peak in the largest city, New York. But it is noteworthy that New York City was 26th in the rate of reported burglary. In sum, we find a strong but less than perfect trend of higher crime in larger cities.

Regional and State Variation

A second striking feature of crime in the U.S. is the variation found from region to region and in some cases from state to state. Recall that crime rates in Canada tended to be higher in the western provinces. The same pattern holds for the U.S. The highest regional crime rates are in the Pacific states (including Hawaii.) The western mountain states tend to have the second highest total crime rates. Particularly low rates are found in the central southern states (Kentucky, Tennessee, Alabama, Mississippi, Arkansas), the midwestern area (Iowa, North and South Dakota, Nebraska) and northern New England (Maine, New Hampshire and Vermont).

These regional patterns break down somewhat when the separate crime items are examined. For example, while central southern states tend to be low overall they have the highest murder rates. In 1983 murder rates ranged from 1.7 in Minnesota and 2.0 in New Hampshire to 14.2 in Texas. Of course, within states there also is a great deal of variation. The highest metropolitan murder rate (23.7) was for the Dade County, Florida, area (Miami), which was closely followed by New Orleans (22.5). These rates are many times higher than rates found in the less urbanized areas of those states. Assault tended to be highest in Florida, New Mexico, and South Carolina. Larceny-theft rates ranged from over 4,200 in Colorado to less than 1,400 in West Virginia. Given these wide variations by region and by state, it is important for local administrators to be aware of the crime patterns in their area.

Offender and Victim Characteristics

Age of offenders. Two major offender characteristics will be considered here. Crime patterns related to age and sex are similar to those found in both Canada and Great Britain. The peak age for committing offenses in the U.S. (based on arrest reports) is for 16 to 20 year olds. For property crimes arrests tend toward the lower end of the 16-20 range, while for violent crimes the trend is toward the upper end. In 1975 offenders under the age of 18 comprised about 25% of all arrests. This proportion has dropped continuously in the last 10 years. In 1983 the proportion of arrests for those under 18 was 17%. There is, however, wide variation between crimes. For example, according to 1981 statistics, 19% of those arrested for violent crimes were under 18, but this group comprised 37% of the arrests for property crimes. Only 9% of murders, but over 40% of burglaries, auto theft and arson were allegedly committed by offenders under 18. Another way of describing the same pattern is to point out that while 16-21 year olds make up about 11% of the population, they account for 32% of all arrests.

Age of victims. There are significant variations related to the age of victims as well as offenders. The peak age of victimization for rape, robbery and aggravated assault is between 16-19. The crimes of larceny and simple assault peak for 20-24 year olds. Most crimes continue to decrease in frequency as the age of the victim increases. With the exception of some forms of larceny those over 65 have the lowest rate of being victimized.

Sex of offenders. In the United States, as elsewhere, males are far more likely than females to commit and be arrested for crimes. While over 80% of all arrests are of males, the proportion varies by type of crime. About 6% of those arrested for burglary are women, but the proportion rises to 13% for murder and 30% for larceny. Women comprise a significant share of the arrests for fraud (41%), embezzlement (29%) and forgery (32%). Over half of those arrested as runaways are female.

Sex of victims. Men are more likely to be victims of crime as well. The 1981 victimization surveys found that robbery rates were 983 for males and 519 for females. Similarly assaults were higher for males (3,623) than for females (1,845). The exceptions were sexual assaults and personal larceny with contact (often purse snatching).

PROCEDURE

The research on crime and disruption in U.S. public libraries actually was the first of the national studies. It was a multi-stage project consisting of several pilot studies to refine the survey instrument, followed by four separate samplings of about 12 states each. Pilot studies were conducted between 1978 and 1980. State samples were surveyed between October, 1981, and June, 1983. Except for several low population states, a systematic sample of at least 60 public libraries in each state was selected for study. A complete listing of all public libraries was obtained from the American Library Directory. To arrive at an unbiased selection of 60 libraries every "nth" library from the state list was selected. The "n" was deter mined by dividing the total number of public libraries by 60. Just over 3,000 library directors were mailed a survey, cover letter and addressed envelope for returns. A more complete description of the procedure is available in an earlier publication (Lincoln, 1984a).

CHARACTERISTICS OF SAMPLE

How does the U.S. sample compare with the samples from Canada and Great Britain? A breakdown shows that in the U.S., sample cities of under 50,000 represented over three quarters of the returns. These came from towns with a population of less than 2,500 (28%), cities of 2,500-10,000 (31%) and cities of 10,000-50,000 (26%). Only 9% of the returns were from cities of over 100,000. As can be seen in Table 4.2, this sample more closely resembles the Canadian sample than the one from Great Britain. Comparisons of crime patterns between the countries should include controls for city size and other factors that differentiate the samples. For example, if the reader compares the amount of book theft in English and American libraries, the comparison should include book theft rates from libraries in cities of comparable size.

The activity level of the library has been suggested as a factor influencing the type and amount of crime. The U.S. sample ranged from libraries reporting fewer than 10 patrons per day (6%) up to libraries daily servicing over 250 patrons (16%). The largest category of library recorded between 51-100 patrons. The U.S. sample contains libraries with lower levels of patron activity than that of libraries in Great Britain, but roughly equivalent to that of Canadian libraries (See Table 4.3). The second indicator of activity level is annual circulation. The most common response here was circulation

Table 4.2

City Size of Sampled Libraries

City Size	U.S.A.	Canada	Great Britain
<2,500	28%	32%	01%
2.5-10,000	31	28	11
10-50,000	26	19	28
50-100,000	06	09	16
100-500,000	06	08	35
>500,000	03	05	10

Table 4.3

Average Number of Patrons Per Day

# Patrons/Day	U.S.A.	Canada	Great Britain
1-10	05%	06%	00%
11-20	10	13	00
21-30	10	10	00
31-50	17	15	02
51-100	22	18	07
101-250	20	21	23
>250	16	18	67

in excess of 99,000 (31%). At the other extreme, 9% of the returns were from libraries circulating fewer than 5,000 items per year. Once again the Canadian and U.S. samples are very similar. Thirty-four percent of Canadian libraries circulated over 99,000 items. In contrast, over 80% of the British sample reported circulation over 99,000.

Employee profiles are the final sample characteristic to be compared. Over 40% of the sample had only one professional librarian. An additional 20% had two staff librarians. Only 3% of the respondents indicated that more than 20 librarians were on the staff. More than half of the sample had fewer than 6 full-time employees of any kind. The average number of librarians was 3.5. Canadian libraries tended to have a slightly smaller professional staff, with 3 librarians in the average library. The typical library in the Great Britain sample employed 11 professionals.

COMPARATIVE PATTERNS OF CRIME

Since the patterns of crime and disruption in U.S. libraries have been described in detail elsewhere (Lincoln and Lincoln 1981; Lincoln 1984a; 1984b), a brief description of the patterns will be included here. The major emphasis at this time will be on examining the similarities and differences between the three national studies. The comparisons between Canadian and U.S. libraries are easy to make since both samples are representative of the full population of public libraries and, as shown above, are similar in important institutional characteristics. The sample from Great Britain is of larger and busier libraries than typically found in the other studies. The description of the crime patterns will emphasize the U.S. and Canadian comparisons first and this will be followed by a comparison of all three national studies using a subsample of libraries that are matched by city size. This will alleviate the problem of comparing the U.S./Canadian samples with the larger, more active British libraries. The U.S. study assessed patterns of 18 different crimes and acts of disruption. Several items were added to the subsequent national surveys, but the same general categories were studied: vandalism/destruction, theft, problem patron behavior, and assault.

Vandalism/Destruction

Intentional book damage. The majority (64%) of U.S. libraries reported book damage. Most of these had repeated episodes, with

28% having chronic problems (6 or more cases per year). The rate of book damage was 526/100. Table 4.4 shows the comparative rates of crimes (per hundred libraries) for each of the nations studied. The rates for Great Britain are presented here for illustrative purposes since these rates are based on the full sample without regard for city size or library activity level.

We have some vandalism to books and catalog equipment. Often the book vandalism is perpetrated when the books are on loan. There is no known remedy.

Vandalism outside the building. Just over half of all returns (54%) indicated that they had some vandalism to the outside of the

Table 4.4

Comparative Rates (per 100) of Crime

Type of Crime	Country		
	U.S.[a]	Canada[a]	G.B.[b]
Book damage	526	655	986
Vandalism outside	215	173	575
Vandalism inside	222	132	348
Vand. equipment	65	39	101
Vand. staff car	38	25	31
Vand. patron car	36	18	43
Arson	7	5	21
Book theft	1,041	982	1,655
Reference theft	443	414	739
A.V. theft	*	53	340
Equipment theft	70	39	166
Fraudulent bills	*	16	33
Counterfeit money	*	9	60
Personal theft	*	57	156
Other theft	137	76	292
Break and enter	*	30	136
Drug use	78	39	80
Drug sales	19	11	20
Harass patron	119	87	329
Harass staff	255	251	672
Obscene phone	*	96	132
Indecent exposure	53	30	41
Assault on patron	14	10	23
Assault on staff	6	6	27
Indices:			
Vandalism	1,069	1,035	2,072
Theft	1,616	1,641	3,498
Problem	459	480	1,235
Assault	19	17	49
TOTAL	2,867	2,995	6,922

a. Representative samples.
b. Sample of central and district libraries.
*. Not included in survey.

library. This was a chronic problem in 10% of the libraries. The rate of vandalism outside the facility was 215. The corresponding Canadian rate was 173.

> Our main problems are not of a serious criminal nature but mainly concerned with vandalism. The library is built on a site frequented by teenagers, and there are few facilities for young people in this area. When the library was first built windows were always being broken, particularly on the weekend when the library was closed. External graffiti is also a problem.

Vandalism inside the building. The rate of known vandalism inside the library (222) was similar to that of vandalism outside the library (215). Just under half of all libraries (45%) had at least one act of interior vandalism during the year. Just over 10% had 6 or more acts. Canadian returns indicated a lower rate (132).

> We have problems with defacement of library furniture — cutting, scratching, etc. We suspect that a few juveniles are responsible for a number of thefts and defacement of property.

Vandalism to cars. Neither damage to patrons' cars nor staff owned cars was very common. Less than 15% reported patrons' cars being vandalized. Most of these cases were isolated incidents, but 7% had repeated occurrences. Similarly, 17% of the respondents knew of damage to a car owned by a staff member, with 8% having repeated problems. The rate for damage to patrons' cars (36) was almost the same as for staff-owned vehicles (38). The rates are substantially higher than those found in the Canadian libraries (patron-owned = 18, staff-owned = 25). Furthermore, despite the fact that the British libraries were in larger cities and served more patrons, the corresponding rates are only slightly higher for patrons' cars (43) and lower for staff-owned cars (31).

Vandalism to equipment. Nearly one-fifth (18%) of the returns told of equipment being intentionally damaged. This occurred 3 or more times in just 7% of the libraries. Equipment was vandalized at a rate of 65/100 libraries, substantially higher than the rate in Canada (39).

Arson. Fortunately, arson is not a common occurrence in libraries. However, during the year, 5% of the U.S. sample reported an act of arson. Most such acts occurred only once. The 5% figure represents 71 libraries that reported arson. Since some of these libraries had multiple episodes, the total number of cases of arson was just over 100. The U.S. rate of arson (7/100) is slightly higher than that found in Canada (5/100).

Vandalism/destruction index. Fewer than 20% of all libraries in the sample were free from vandalism. Over 70% had at least 2 episodes, and 30% had 10 or more. One of 20 libraries had over 40 acts of vandalism per year. The average number of incidents per library was 10.7, a rate per hundred of 1,069, which is almost identical to the Canadian rate of 1,035.

Theft

Books. The theft of books was the most common crime. Exactly 80% of the returns mentioned book theft. Over half of the cases had chronic problems (6 or more cases), while 27% of this sample had more than 20 repetitions. The average number of separate episodes of book theft (not the same as the number of stolen volumes) was 10.4. Many respondents indicated that single patrons were responsible for the loss of numerous volumes at one time. The rate of book theft (1,041) was slightly higher than that tabulated for Canada (982). The larger British libraries experienced rates of over 1,650.

> We are plagued with the theft of monograph materials.
>
> There are many attempts to steal books. Some borrowers have identified tags and tear them out.
>
> Our most serious problem is book theft. No statistics exist to give true costs, but predation in popular subject areas is very evident. Particularly in those subjects popular with children and teenagers.

Reference material. The second most common type of theft involved the loss of reference materials. Approximately two-thirds (63%) of the sample had reference materials stolen. Over 20% had at least six episodes. The rate of reference theft (443) was similar to the Canadian rate (414). British libraries reported a substantially higher rate (739).

Equipment. Less than a quarter of our returns listed the theft of equipment. Twelve percent had two or more equipment losses. The rate of equipment theft was 70 per 100 libraries in the U.S. and 39 in Canada.

Other theft. In an attempt to assess additional thefts that were not specifically measured, a summary category of "other theft" was included in the U.S. survey. For the studies of Canadian and Great Britain's libraries, some of the additional theft categories were included in the survey. Approximately one third of the U.S. respondents reported other theft. Twenty percent had 2 or more acts, while 5% had chronic problems. The U.S. rate of other theft was 137 compared with the Canadian rate of 76. The low Canadian rate is probably due to the fact that the category of "other theft" was more limited since the additional specific crimes (i.e., personal and AV theft) were included in the survey.

> The only crime which has any effect is the theft of records, which is sporadic.
>
> We've had thefts of unattended bags, etc. belonging to browsing borrowers. Notices are posted and verbal warnings given users not to leave their property unattended even for the briefest period.

Theft index. How often did thefts occur in the library? Over 80% of returns indicated at least one theft, with the majority (60%) reporting 6 or more repetitions. There were over 50 separate thefts annually in 6% of the sample. The average number of thefts was 16.2, or a rate of 1,616. A comparable rate of theft was found in Canada (1,641).

Problem Patron Behavior

Drug use and sales. The overwhelming majority of librarians were not aware of any drug sales in the building. This is a difficult crime to measure since contact leading to sales would be made when surveillance was unlikely. Only 4% of the sample reported that drugs were being sold in the building. In over half of the cases where drug sales were apparent, there tended to be repeated problems. The rate of drug sales was 19 in the U.S., 11 in Canada and 20 in Great Britain. Note that the rate in Great Britain's larger, busier libraries was basically the same as the U.S. rate.

Drug use was more frequent than drug sales. Slightly more than

15% of the returns mentioned drug use in the library. Again, this was a problem that tended to be repeated, if it occurred at all. Ten percent had two or more cases of drug use by staff or patrons. The rates of known drug use were 78/100 in the U.S., exactly twice the Canadian rate and similar to the rate in Great Britain (80).

Verbal abuse to patron. About 1 of 4 libraries (28%) reported abuse of a patron. In 10% this was an isolated incident, but it occurred 3 or more times in 12% of the sampled institutions. The rate of verbal abuse to patrons was higher in the U.S. (119) than in Canada (87). A substantially higher rate was reported by the sampled British libraries (329).

> Our main problems occur during winter evenings and involve disruptive behavior by groups of young people within the 12-18 age group. Behavior is mainly the result of high spirits and boredom—but they can be obnoxious to users.

Verbal abuse of staff. This was one of the most common problems reported. Almost half (45%) of the returns indicated that a staff member had been verbally abused. In 13% of the libraries verbal abuse of the staff was chronic (6 times or more). The rates of staff abuse were equivalent in Canada (251) and the United States (255).

> Most abuse comes from young teenagers who make a nuisance of themselves while they are using the library as a place to keep warm. We throw them out and bar the ringleaders from future library use.

Indecent exposure. Activities defined by respondents as indecent exposure occurred in almost one fifth (18%) of the sample. The problem was an isolated episode in half of these cases. Chronic acts of indecent exposure occurred in only 2% of the libraries. The United States had the highest rate (53), followed by the British sample (41) and the Canadian sample (30).

Problem patron index. The majority of respondents (53%) told of at least one incident involving a problem patron. Remember that the definition of problem patron includes only drug related behavior, harassment, and indecent exposure. The other "problems" caused by patrons are included within the other categories of crime and disruption. Ten percent of the returns mentioned a single event, but

43% had 2 or more experiences with a problem patron. Ten percent also had over a dozen cases. There were over 25 separate instances in 5% of the sampled libraries. The U.S. rate of problem patron behavior was 459, slightly lower than the Canadian rate of 480. However, the Canadian rate includes obscene phone calls in addition to the other problems. When these problems are excluded from the rate, then the comparable rate for Canada was under 400.

> So many problems can be caused by one person. A problem child now growing into a problem teenager lives immediately across the street from the library and has been the cause of much trouble.

Assault. Assaults on patrons were more than twice as common as assaults on staff. While 7% of the sample told of assaults against a patron only 3% knew of a staff member being assaulted. Patron assaults occurred more than once in just 2% of the sample, and multiple staff assaults also were rare (1%). Although the percentages are low, they indicate that over 100 U.S. libraries reported a patron assault and more than 50 reported a staff assault. The rates were 14/100 (patron) and 6/100 (staff). Combining the two assault items shows that almost 10% of the sample had some type of assault. Six percent had a single experience, and 3% had multiple assaults. Similar patterns were found in Canada. Assaults against patrons were almost twice as likely to occur as were assaults against the staff. A strikingly different pattern is shown for the British libraries. First of all, the rates are higher, as would be expected for these larger libraries. However, the rate of assault against a staff member (27) was slightly higher than the rate against a patron (23).

Total crime and disruption. It was the unusual library (11%) that reported no problems. Two-thirds had 6 or more incidents during the year. One quarter of the sample had more than 40 episodes of crime or disruption. The high crime libraries, those in the highest 10%, each reported a minimum of 75 separate incidents. The average total number of reported episodes of crime and disruption was 28.7. The rate per 100 libraries was 2,867. When the Canadian rates are adjusted to contain only items identical to those in the U.S. survey, then the total rate was under 2,800, while the overall Canadian rate was 2,995. The Total Index for Great Britain's libraries approached 7,000. However, as mentioned above, it is important to compare similar libraries when examining cross-cultural patterns of crime. These comparisons will be made in detail when describing the relationships between city size and crime.

INSTITUTIONAL FACTORS RELATED TO CRIME

Both the Canadian and British studies described in Chapters Two and Three identified significant relationships between several characteristics of the library and the level of crime. Are there similar patterns for the U.S. study? As will be shown, the general answer is yes. The associations between crime and factors such as circulation levels, number of patrons, and staff size are evident in all three studies.

Circulation. The level of circulation was positively related to each of the crime items. The weakest links were with arson, drug sales and staff assaults. The strongest associations were with the level of book theft, book damage and reference theft. Each of the indices was likewise affected by the level of circulation. It was interesting to note that the likelihood of having chronic problems with the various types of crime also was related to circulation level. For example, chronic book theft and reference theft increased consistently as the level of circulation increased. While only 32% of libraries with a circulation of under 5,000 had three or more episodes of book theft, this level was reported by over 90% of the libraries with a circulation of at least 99,000. In some cases the increase in crime as circulation increases is substantial. For example, the book theft rate in libraries circulating fewer than 5,000 items was 340/100, but this rose continuously to 1,797/100 in libraries with a circulation in excess of 99,000. Total crime increased from 759 (< 5,000) to 1,962 (26-50,000) and 5,887 (> 99,000).

Number of patrons. Once again each of the crime items, except drug sales, was positively related to the number of patrons using the library. The highest correlations again were for reference theft, book theft and intentional book damage. The lowest correlations were with drug sales, staff assault and arson. These tend to be the more serious crimes, the ones where possible witnesses would be a deterrent. When city size was used as a control, allowing for a comparison of the effect of patron activity within cities of the same size, most of the correlations were still significant. However, arson and assault were no longer related to the number of patrons. That is, within comparable cities the level of these crimes did not increase as the number of patrons increased. This may imply that having large numbers of patrons either acts as a deterrent to these crimes or conversely that high rates of the crimes deters patrons from using the library. Either of these possible relationships would account for the nonsignificant correlations. The rate of each of the crimes for selected patron activity levels is shown in Table 4.5.

Staff size. The pattern of crime as a function of staff size is clear. As the size of the professional staff increases, the level of crime increases as well. Each of the crime items is significantly related to staff size. The strongest correlations were for reference theft and book theft. For example, among libraries with only 1 librarian, 57% reported some book theft. In those libraries with 3 or more professional staff over 90% had book theft. Similar patterns were found for most of the other crimes. In sum, the various indicators of the activity level of the library—circulation, number of patrons and

Table 4.5

Crime Rates as a Function of Patron Activity Level

Type of Episode	Number of Patrons				
	<10	31-50	51-100	101-250	>250
Book damage	109	283	451	814	1,235
Vandalism outside	80	116	182	288	469
Vandalism inside	45	92	192	285	615
Equipment damage	6	11	47	87	197
Damage staff car	0	15	21	52	115
Damage patron car	3	17	34	38	115
Arson	0	2	3	16	18
Book theft	346	662	1,065	1,517	1,997
Reference theft	39	190	338	662	1,142
Equipment theft	12	24	50	59	206
Other theft	9	86	116	163	342
Drug use	1	32	47	125	219
Drug sales	0	2	4	23	88
Harassed patron	4	52	68	164	364
Harassed staff	16	110	174	390	703
Indecent exposure	20	8	27	86	197
Assault on patron	0	4	4	21	44
Assault on staff	0	3	2	10	20
INDICES:					
Vandalism	239	520	928	1,473	2,719
Theft	416	930	1,583	2,360	3,693
Problem Patron	41	185	318	716	1,456
Assault	0	7	6	30	62
Total	672	1,572	2,801	4,332	7,642

staff size—all show that as activity increases the level of most crimes in the library also increases.

COMMUNITY FACTORS AFFECTING CRIME

City size. At the beginning of this chapter it was pointed out that there are prominent differences in the crime rates found in cities of different sizes. This also is true of crime affecting libraries. The correlations between crime level and city size were among the highest found. These ranged from r. = .54 for reference theft to r. = .15 for assault against staff. All of the indices were strongly associated (above r. = .50) with the size of the city. The differences in some of the crime rates are striking. The rate of book theft ranged from 429 for towns of under 2,500, to 1,542 for cities of 10-50,000, to 1,755 for cities of over 500,000. The serious crimes showed similar continuous increases (see Table 4.6). For example, the arson rate increased from .5 in the smallest towns to 37 in the large cities. Examination of the indices shows that theft increased from 531/100 in towns of below 2,500 to 3,641 in the largest cities. Vandalism showed similar patterns of increase in U.S. libraries—from 282/100 in towns of under 2,500 to 2,611 in cities of over a half million. The assault rate increased nearly thirty-fold from 3/100 (under 2,500) to 84/100 (over 500,000). There were steady increases in the total amount of crime as well. The lowest rates were found in the smallest towns (790/100), increasing to over 4,500 in cities of 10-50,000 and peaking at nearly 7,000 in the largest cities. These general increases appear in each of the national studies conducted.

> This is of very little consequence to us in a small town, where staff have good relations with readers and community. Damage to books by careless readers, or willful damage in a few cases plus nonreturn of books, these are our most serious problems.

Comparative rates for library crime and disruption in similar sized cities are shown in Table 4.7. These figures provide the best comparisons of the differences and similarities between the three studies. Notice that data from two different population areas are presented. Additional comparisons can be made by referring to Ta-

Table 4.6

Crime Rates as a Function of City Size

Type of Episode	<2.5	2.5-10	10-50	50-100	100-500	>500
Book damage	155	353	854	1,019	1,070	1,184
Vandalism outside	81	140	319	428	423	616
Vandalism inside	42	125	412	543	357	508
Equipment damage	14	22	113	174	129	153
Damage staff car	6	16	59	87	87	155
Damage patron car	2	15	64	101	86	106
Arson	1	3	13	14	7	37
Book theft	429	848	1,542	1,839	1,689	1,754
Reference theft	85	242	718	1,036	936	1,174
Equipment theft	12	46	93	108	169	284
Other theft	39	106	184	167	333	482
Drug use	9	55	92	239	295	117
Drug sales	0	4	26	33	65	72
Harassed patron	18	48	162	284	390	468
Harassed staff	45	124	433	555	726	682
Indecent exposure	13	21	58	167	149	276
Assault on patron	2	4	20	28	46	64
Assault on staff	1	2	13	6	18	20
INDICES:						
Vandalism	282	670	1,765	2,165	2,190	2,611
Theft	531	1,194	2,418	3,078	3,142	3,641
Problem Patron	72	236	678	1,210	1,413	1,411
Assault	3	6	31	34	63	84
Total	799	1,999	4,595	6,048	6,482	6,946

bles 2.10, 3.7 and 4.6. Starting with the Total Index, it is clear that the highest level of reported crime is from Great Britain's libraries. In cities of 50-100,000, the lowest total rates were in the U.S. libraries (6,048), followed by Canadian Libraries (6,870), and peaking in Great Britain's institutions (7,495). Even if the individual crime items not examined in the U.S. study are deleted, Great Britain still has the highest rate. Also, recall that many of these crimes were reported by American respondents in the "other theft" category. The same ordering of crime rates is found in the cities of 100-500,000: Great Britain, 9,082; Canada, 8,238; U.S., 6,481. U.S. libraries did show the highest levels of assaults and problem patron behavior in cities of between 50-100,000. However, in the larger cities the problems were more pronounced in British libraries.

There are important differences between the national rates for the specific crimes as well. For example, book theft rates in cities of 50-100,000 were comparable (U.S.: 1,839; Canada: 1,737; G.B.: 1,890), but in the larger cities the U.S. rates dropped somewhat

(U.S.: 1,689; Canada: 1,847; G.B.: 1,907). Verbal abuse of staff was remarkably similar in cities of 50-100,000. The rates were 555/100 in the U.S., 503/100 in Canada and 510/100 in Great Britain. Rates in the larger cities each showed an increase and national differences (U.S.: 726; Canada: 808; G.B.: 933).

In several cases there were consistent national differences. For example, book damage was higher in Canadian libraries for both city categories. Vandalism outside the building, arson and assault against staff were more likely to be reported by British libraries. Drug use and indecent exposure were much more common in U.S. libraries.

Location of schools and police stations. Does being close to schools affect the level of crime in the library? To some degree it does. Since city size has been shown to influence crime rates, the

Table 4.7

City Size and Comparative Crime Rates

	CITY:	50-100,000			100-500,000	
Type of Episode	U.S.A.	Canada	G.B.	U.S.A.	Canada	G.B.
Book damage	1,019	1,449	1,132	1,070	1,500	1,205
Vandalism outside	428	262	570	423	287	828
Vandalism inside	543	279	245	357	353	472
Equipment damage	174	116	110	129	105	119
Damage staff car	87	64	39	87	121	38
Damage patron car	101	35	16	86	58	94
Arson	14	14	26	7	8	28
Book theft	1,839	1,737	1,890	1,689	1,847	1,907
Reference theft	1,036	1,239	982	936	900	973
A V theft		141	445		200	278
Equipment theft	108	103	283	169	127	259
Fraudulent bill		38	65		7	33
Counterfeit money		7	16		3	90
Personal theft		152	269		160	181
Other theft	167	118	120	333	150	439
Forced entry		52	83		39	207
Drug use	239	38	10	295	171	196
Drug sales	33	2	52	65	92	34
Harassed patron	284	119	252	390	235	457
Harassed staff	555	503	510	726	808	933
Obscene calls		204	30		431	220
Indecent exposure	167	121	10	149	84	59
Assault on patron	28	10	3	46	24	50
Assault on staff	6	10	13	18	2	49
INDICES:						
Vandalism	2,165	2,282	2,136	2,190	2,432	2,762
Theft	3,078	3,773	4,217	3,142	3,861	4,280
Problem Patron	1,210	932	861	1,413	1,614	1,797
Assault	34	21	17	63	26	95
Total	6,048	6,870	7,495	6,482	8,238	9,082

effect of school location should be examined with controls on population level. Within small towns (under 2,500) there is greater book damage, reference theft, verbal abuse, and vandalism when the library is in the same block as the junior high school. The effects are not as striking when a senior high school is on the same block as the library. In cities of 50,000 and more, the proximity of the school has less of an impact on the level of crime in the library.

> There are so many students nearby that we are always having problems with vandalism. We have tried to alleviate the problem by aiming to interest the children and teenagers in USING the library and having activities during the school-holidays. The staff are friendly and helpful but use discipline when necessary. This would appear to show rewards since over the last two years vandalism has decreased greatly.

An ideal deterrent to crime would be constant potential surveillance by police. When police stations are located in the same block as the library, this is basically what happens. In the small towns there was a substantially lower rate of book theft, reference theft, vandalism and abuse when the police station was very close to the library than when it was not. In large cities, the crimes occurring inside the library were not affected by the proximity of police stations. However, vandalism outside the building was lower when the police were nearby.

COST OF CRIME

The U.S. survey contained several indicators of the cost of crime. Respondents were asked about both their actual losses from crime and changes in service to the public. As in earlier chapters, the institutional costs will be examined first, followed by a discussion of the effects upon the staff members.

Institutional Costs

Financial losses. Losses of over $1,000 were reported by 22 of the sample. This was about the same proportion that reported losses of under $100. An additional 12% indicated that they had no losses at all. The level of loss was related to a number of factors, including city size (r. = .56), number of patrons (r. = .51) and circulation level (r. = 59). The average loss in towns of under 2,500 was just over $100. In contrast, cities over 50,000 had average losses of nearly $1,000. These losses were slightly higher than in the Canadian libraries. As expected the losses in the sample of British central and district libraries were higher, but when library activity is controlled for then the loss levels are more comparable. The average loss level in libraries with between 101 and 250 patrons per day was just under $500 in the U.S., close to $300 in Canada and approximately 200 pounds in Great Britain. In the most active libraries (over 1,000 patrons/day) the average loss in Great Britain was over 500 pounds.

Crime prevention expenses. The financial losses described above are considered direct costs of crime. They are the result of specific episodes of crime and disruption. Along with these costs are the indirect costs resulting from fear of subsequent crime. Annual crime prevention expenses are a good example. It is clear from the survey results that budgeting for crime prevention is not common in American public libraries. Three quarters of the sample spent nothing on crime prevention in the 12 months prior to receiving the survey. This included 34% of the libraries falling into the high crime category. This point should be emphasized. Among the libraries with the highest levels of crime, 1 out of 3 spent nothing on crime prevention.

One of the interesting findings related to crime prevention expenses was that there was a very strong relationship between the level of verbal abuse to staff and prevention expenditures. Of all the crime and disruption items this showed the strongest association (r. = .38). It appears that staff harassment facilitates decisions to commit funds for crime prevention.

Crime prevention costs can be compared across the studies. Overall, average crime prevention expenses were highest in Great Britain. But this is not surprising, given the nature of that sample. Half of the respondents indicated that there were no ongoing prevention expenses, and about 15% reported over 1,000 pounds. In Canada (74%) and the United States (74%) higher proportions indicated no expense. In Canada only 4% had expenses exceeding $2,500 (roughly equivalent to 1,000 pounds), while in the U.S. 7% had expenses at that level. Adding the control for library size, we find that the average crime prevention expenses in libraries serving over 250 patrons per day were higher in the U.S. ($260) than in Great

Britain (125 pounds) or Canada ($230, Canadian). In larger cities (100-500,000) crime prevention expenditures in the U.S. and Canada were lower than those in Great Britain.

Total expenses. Ten percent of the libraries reported no losses and no crime prevention expenses. At the other extreme, about 4% had combined losses and prevention expenses in excess of $10,000. Total crime related expenses increased dramatically as the number of patrons increased.

Closed the library. The most obvious effect of crime on the library would be to close the building. Only a few libraries (2%) had to close because of crime. Most of these closed only once during the year. This is the same proportion as found in the Canadian study. Several of the crime items, particularly the various forms of vandalism and indecent exposure, were associated with a forced closing. Even fewer U.S. libraries (1.2%) closed a branch because of problems with crime (see Table 4.8).

Changing schedule. A less dramatic, but sometimes effective, response to crime is to change the operating schedule. If an assessment of crime problems indicates that there are high risk times for crime, then schedule changes may be a viable option. Nearly 4% of the responses included a change in schedule in an attempt to control crime. This is substantially lower than the British sample (9%) and slightly higher than the Canadian sample (2%). Schedule changes

Table 4.8

Personal and Institutional Effects of Crime

Institutional Impact:	Rate per 100 Libraries		
	U.S.A.	Canada	G.B.
Closed library	2	3	9
Closed branch library	2	2	11
Changed operating hours	4	3	11
Lost use of equipment	15	11	18
Stopped community programs	10	10	8
Called police	97	90	200
Training session	18	14	30
Staff Impact:	Proportion Reporting		
	U.S.A.	Canada	G.B.
Avoid work after dark	7%	3%	14%
Picked up after work	9%	10%	18%
Escorted to car	17%	10%	18%

were most closely associated with vandalism outside the building and drug problems.

> The change in hours prevented any further assaults on librarians.

> A while ago there was a real problem in the library with teenagers. This became a hangout for them, and they gave the staff considerable grief. As a result the librarian cut the night hours and publicized the reason for her doing so in the paper.

Lost use of equipment. Just under 10% of the U.S. libraries operated without equipment that had been stolen or intentionally damaged. The losses occurred more than one time in about half of the affected libraries. These findings are similar to those from the other national samples. In total, 123 U.S. libraries reported that they were without equipment that had been damaged or stolen. This figure is substantially lower than the number of libraries reporting theft (335) or damage (297) to equipment. Thus it appears that most libraries repair and/or replace equipment that is inoperable. The actual costs of this replacement and repair should be considered direct costs against the operating budget.

Stopped programs. Another response to crime that may be noticeable to the public is to curtail community programs. One in 20 libraries voluntarily stopped community programs. Half of these discontinued one program, while half stopped 2 or more. The decision to stop programs was closely associated with the level of damage and theft of equipment and verbal abuse of the staff. Several institutional and community factors also were associated with discontinuing programs, including city size and circulation level. Each of the three national studies found that 5% of the sample had stopped community programs.

Called police. Comparatively few libraries were forced to close, change schedules or discontinue programs. On the other hand, 45% had called police at least once during the year. The majority of these had called more than once. The decision to call police was most strongly associated with high levels of verbal abuse of the staff. The level of vandalism inside and outside the facility also were good predictors of requesting police assistance, as were city size, circulation level and the number of patrons served. Once again we find that the patterns of requesting police assistance are similar in the U.S.

and Canada. British libraries were more likely (73%) to have called in the police.

> We have made attempts to get regular visits from police. Some difficulties on their part in maintaining the regular visits.
>
> The branch library is located within a small park in a suburban residential area. Local teenagers gather in the park in the evenings, and drug and alcohol consumption occur. The police have had to get involved because of subsequent vandalism.

Institutional impact. Combining the answers to questions about the impact of crime on the library (closing, schedule changes, lost equipment and stopped programs) gives an indicator of the institutional impact of crime. Nearly 1 in 10 respondents reported one of these effects. An additional 7% had multiple effects of crime. If "calling the police" is added to the index, then almost half (48%) indicated institutional effects of crime. Multiple effects were reported by 31%.

Effect on services. We have already described the actual effects of crime such as closing the building. An item also measured the respondent's perception of how much crime affected the services to the public. For the most part it appears that crime is not perceived to cause serious problems with regard to providing service. Two-fifths indicated that there was no effect of crime on the ability to serve the public, while nearly half (46%) said that there was very little effect. However, 11% felt that services were affected moderately and 2% a great deal. These perceptions are quite similar to those of Canadian library administrators. The perceived severity of impact was related closely to the level of book damage, book theft, reference theft and verbal abuse of the staff.

Personal costs. Crime impacts upon the staff and patrons as well as upon the functioning of the institution. Voluntary and institutionally implemented changes in the behavior of the staff resulting from a concern with crime were examined. Five percent of the sample indicated that they carried some type of protective device while at work. A similar proportion (7%) claimed that they knew of at least one of their colleagues who did so. Twenty-one percent of the respondents said that they personally had been the victim of a crime while working in the library. Nearly a third of these cases involved repeated crime. Men were about twice as likely to be victims as were women who worked in the library. Librarians who had been victimized in a library setting were more likely to carry protection devices than nonvictimized staff. For example, 2% of nonvictimized staff compared with 6% of twice victimized and 17% of those victimized 3 or more times carried personal protection items. Women were twice as likely as men to carry such devices. In fact, among the men only the victimized subsample carried protection. Virtually none of the Canadian respondents indicated that they had protective devices with them at work.

A number of respondents (7%) indicated that they personally avoided working after dark. Female employees were more likely to avoid evening work as were those who had been the victim of more than one crime in the library. A single victimization apparently did not increase the likelihood of avoiding evening hours. Crime prevention behavior might also include avoiding isolation during times of risk. We asked whether respondents were picked up at work. Just under 10% indicated that they were picked up as a safety procedure, with men (10%) being somewhat more likely than women (7%) to be picked up. Being the victim of a crime increased the likelihood of being picked up at work. While 7% of nonvictims arranged for rides, 13% of previously victimized librarians did the same. As can be seen in Table 4.8 the figures for the different national samples show some similarity but several important differences as well. For example, American librarians were more likely than their Canadian counterparts to try to avoid work after dark, but equally likely to be picked up after work. British librarians in the sample were the most likely to avoid work after dark and to be picked up because of concern about crime.

> We require that our high school pages be picked up at night.

> We have gone to the trouble of double staffing so that we'll feel safer during the rush hours.

SUMMARY

The vast majority (about 90%) of crime in the U.S. is property crime. Larceny theft is the most common offense.

Over 2,900 U.S. libraries were included in the systematic sample of public libraries, and 1,657 respondents returned the completed survey.

The most common crimes in the libraries were book and reference theft. The least common crimes were assaults on staff and arson.

The activity level of the library influenced both the type and amount of crime. For example, total crime increased more than ten fold from libraries serving less than 10 patrons per day to those serving over 250 patrons.

City size greatly influenced crime rates in libraries. Arson increased from less than 1 case per 100 libraries in the smallest towns to 37 cases per 100 in the largest cities. Assaults on staff increased by a factor of 20, and patron assaults increased even more.

The theft rates were over 1,600. The total rate of crime exceeded 2,800 incidents per 100 libraries.

Comparisons of the three national studies found that when city size was controlled for, U.S. libraries had more problems with drug use and indecent exposure, Canadian libraries had more problems with damage to books, while British libraries had more problems with vandalism outside the building, arson and assault against staff.

REFERENCES

Gallup, George, The Gallup Poll., June 7, 1979; March 8, 1981, (Princeton, N.J.).
Lincoln, Alan Jay, *Crime in the Library: A Study of Patterns, Impact and Security.* (New York: R. R. Bowker), 1984.
Lincoln, Alan Jay, "Patterns and costs of crime," *Library Trends*, 33:1, (1984):69:76.
Lincoln, Alan Jay and Lincoln, Carol Z., "The impact of crime in public libraries," *Library and Archival Security*, 3, (1980):125-137.
Research and Forecasts Inc., *The Figgie Report on Fear and Crime: America Afraid*, (Willoughby, Ohio: A.T.O. Inc), 1980.

Chapter Five

Patterns of Library Security

In this chapter we will examine several issues related to security in public libraries, including the deployment patterns of various security devices and the implementation of personnel policies. This material will be integrated with information on differences in security use as a function of selected institutional and community characteristics and the comparisons across the three national studies. When possible, the relationship between using security and the level of crime will be examined, and the reported major problems and "solutions" to these major concerns will be illustrated using the actual responses from library administrators.

In earlier chapters the important differences between direct and indirect costs were clarified. It was shown that crime and disruption may result in lost books and materials, damage to the facility and equipment and other direct costs. Each of these crimes results in some financial cost that is either ignored (books and materials not replaced, equipment not repaired, etc.) or covered by the operating budget or through special allocations. Various indirect costs of crimes, such as the carrying of protective devices and the avoiding of work at high risk times were also described. Whenever staff or patrons alter behavior because of the anticipation of future crime, they are demonstrating an indirect cost of crime. The use of security devices and crime prevention programs also are direct costs since they are employed in an attempt to reduce and control anticipated crime.

SECURITY IN BRITISH LIBRARIES

Previous studies (Lincoln, 1980, 1984) have shown that the larger libraries typically found in urban areas are more likely to have security programs in place than are smaller, rural libraries. The nature of the British sample suggests that comparatively high levels of security would be found. Later in this chapter cross-cultural comparisons will be shown, but first the reported use of 16 different security options will be examined for Great Britain.

Security in libraries should be viewed as a multifaceted problem. The organizational scheme being used to help analyze security problems in public libraries includes six types of security: (1) property line protection, (2) entry point protection, (3) general interior protection, (4) specific point interior protection, (5) multiple point protection and (6) personnel safety. Although security problems are being considered separately, they may in practice overlap. That is, a program to secure specific points within the library also may function to protect staff. Our concern here is with the primary function of the security item or policy. In the final chapter an extensive security checklist is presented that provides a more comprehensive overview of possible security procedures than was considered of the research projects.

Property Line Protection

Property line protection is the "first line of defense" of the library. It serves to remind both potential intruders and legitimate users that they are entering the territory of the library. Although the property line barriers commonly used by public libraries may not prevent illegal entry to the building, they may function in some cases as a psychological deterrent.

The major survey item that focused on property line protection was the coordination of patrol coverage of the library by local police. Other items (uniformed guards, closed circuit television, etc.) relate to property line protection but not as a primary function. Police patrol on an unpredictable schedule is a useful deterrent to crime. It is relatively unobtrusive but the occasional presence of police can serve to deter intruders, and reassure legitimate users that they are safe.

> Alcoholics and down and outs frequent our library. The book theft detection system prevents their entry to a large extent nowadays, but generally if they will not leave the building quietly, a phone call to the police is usually sufficient to frighten them off. Sometimes the police come by and check on their own.

Among the sampled British libraries, 20% had some type of police patrol coverage (See Table 5.1). The relationship between city size and the use of police patrol was weak. Libraries in cities of all sizes were about equally likely to use patrols. The exception was for libraries in the largest cities (over 500,000), which reported less reliance on patrols (only 12%). The decision to request police patrol was not related to either the level of circulation or the number of patrons using the library. However, it was related to the perceived effect of crime on services. The greater the reported effect of crime, the greater the likelihood of using police patrols. In addition, several of the crime items were related to the use of patrols. Police patrols were more likely when the levels of equipment theft, outside vandalism, vandalism to cars, assault on staff, personal theft and breaking and entering were high. These crimes are not specifically problems of libraries but of any public facility, and are crimes that are commonly referred to police.

One question that should be examined is the relationship between

Table 5.1

Proportion of British Libraries Using Security Options

Type of Measure	Low Crime	High Crime	Total
Police patrol	7%	46%	20%
Security locks	14	64	44
Intrusion alarms (entry)	14	69	36
Security screens	7	46	24
Unbreakable windows	29	64	34
Intrusion alarms (interior)	36	64	36
Smoke/heat detector	14	54	26
Locked storage room	53	85	55
Book theft system	7	33	26
Surveillance cameras	7	8	8
Uniformed guards	0	25	12
Plainclothes guards	0	15	5
Escort for staff	0	39	17
Staff training	0	57	30
Portable alarms	0	8	8
Police communication link	36	57	33
Any of above items	75	100	92
Average number of crimes	6	178	69

the level of crime and the use of security. There are several ways to do this, including comparing the use of security in libraries with the lowest and highest levels of crime. Libraries with total crime scores in the top 10% of the sample were designated as high crime libraries. The 10% with the lowest total crime scores comprised the low crime subsample. Over half (54%) of the libraries reporting the highest amount of crime used police patrols, compared with 7% of the low crime libraries.

Entry Point Protection

If protection at the property line is not sufficient to deter illegal entry, then it is important to have some protection at the actual points of entry. These security options may actually prevent or impede entry, or in some cases merely provide warning that there is (or was) an attempt to enter the facility.

The commonest source of illegal entry to most buildings is through a main door. Secure locks should be considered whenever there is a likelihood of breaking and entering. However, less than half (44%) of the sample reported that they had some type of security lock on outside doors. Thirty percent had a security lock on some entry doors, and 14% had security locks on all doors. Among the high crime libraries, 64% had at least some doors equipped with security locks, compared with only 14% of the low crime libraries. Security locks were slightly more likely to be used in libraries in larger cities and in the more active libraries. They also were likely to be found when vandalism inside the building and AV theft were common.

> We have a very old building to which it is relatively easy to obtain entry. Two major burglaries have occurred in the past year. Vandalism of property and theft of keys took place. A security light system has been incorporated, but we still have had one break-in since this operation.

Intrusion alarms might be considered as part of a security program. These alarms function either by attracting the attention of people passing by or by direct contact with a monitoring agency. We did not differentiate between the two systems. Just over a third of the British sample had intrusion alarms on one or more doors. Half of these libraries had alarms on some of doors, and the other half on all outside doors. Over two-thirds of the high crime libraries had at least some doors secured with intrusion alarms, compared with 13% of low crime libraries. The use of intrusion alarms was only marginally related to city size and patron activity level. It was not related to circulation level. There were strong relationships between the use of intrusion alarms and existing levels of drug sales, vandalism inside the building, AV theft and verbal abuse to patrons. There was a slight tendency for break-ins to be lower when intrusion alarms were in place.

An additional way of protecting entry points is with the use of security screens or unbreakable glass. Approximately one fourth of the libraries had some security screens, and one third had some unbreakable windows. In almost all cases, only some windows were protected. Two thirds of the high crime libraries had some unbreakable windows. Neither the size of the city nor the level of circulation was related to the use of these items. Theft was higher in libraries with some security screens than in libraries without security screens. It may be that when theft is high, the deployment of entry point security does not eliminate the problem, but rather leads to some reduction or at least keeps the problem from increasing even more. This is likely the case when thefts are committed by users who enter the building legally.

> We were subject to window breakage by vandalism and attempted break-ins. We do not have padlocked grills on all doors and windows.

> To deter vandalism we have installed both unbreakable glass and improvements in lighting.

General Interior Protection

Security designed to protect the general interior of the library functions primarily against those illegally in the facility but may be useful against those who entered legitimately but are attempting to gain access to restricted areas. Electronic intrusion alarms such as motion detectors or photoelectric systems are designed to respond to changes in physical conditions in the designated areas. Motion detection systems operate by noting interruptions in either ultrasonic or radio frequency waves picked up by receivers in the area. Audio or sonic alarms respond to noise in the area. The systems can be very effective in detecting intruders.

Over a third of the British libraries had some type of interior intrusion alarm system in place. Among the high crime libraries, 64% had functioning systems. Systems were more likely to be found in the larger city and busier libraries. The level of equipment theft was the crime item most strongly associated with having intrusion alarms. Vandalism inside the building and theft of reference material also was strongly associated with having these systems. That is, the libraries with higher levels of these crimes were most likely to have intrusion alarms.

One of the simplest interior protection devices is a heat or smoke detector. Only 25% of the general sample but 54% of the high crime sample reported using either one. Detectors were more likely to be used in libraries with large circulation and patron activity levels. High levels of vandalism in the building were the factors most strongly associated with having smoke or heat detectors. Among libraries reporting a case of arson, only 29% used a smoke or heat detector. This was almost identical to the 25% deployment of those with no reported arson.

Specific Interior Protection

High risk areas within the library might be appropriate locations for specific interior protection. These are likely to include work areas, exits, bathrooms, stairwells and so on. These areas can be protected by specific security measures or by the more general options described below under multiple point protection. We asked about 2 items used in many libraries, book theft detection systems and locked storage rooms. While the book theft systems reduce theft of items housed in many parts of the building, they do so by securing the exit area(s). Just under one fourth of the libraries used book theft detection systems. They were more common among the high crime libraries (33%) than in low crime libraries (7%). The use of book theft systems also was more common in larger cities and busier libraries and in libraries with higher overall expenses resulting from crime. In cities of under 50,000, approximately 10% used book theft systems, compared to 38% in cities of over 50,000. In addition, the greater the perceived effect of crime on services, the greater the likelihood of having a book theft system. Nearly half (44%) of libraries with crime affecting the public "a great deal" had book theft systems, compared with only 17% of those that reported no effect of crime on services.

Another major problem is the attempted theft of book stock from the reference library. This has been alleviated to a considerable extent by the installation of an anti-book-theft device.

Book, and particularly cassette theft, is a continuing problem. The latter, especially, has not been solved by the installation of a theft detection system.

The level of book theft, as measured by the number of volumes stolen, was influenced by the presence of book theft systems. In libraries with systems in place, 38% reported fewer than 25 volumes stolen during the year. Among libraries without a system a nearly identical proportion (37%) had fewer than 25 stolen volumes. Considering that the libraries with systems had considerably larger collections with higher levels of circulation, this is a reassuring finding. The use of book theft systems appears to control theft in a sizable proportion of the facilities. However, the average number of stolen volumes from libraries without theft systems was 203. In contrast, libraries with theft systems reported an average loss of 441 volumes. Nearly a quarter of the responses indicated that despite the deployment of a book theft system total losses of books and serials still exceeded 1,000 volumes. But when the activity level of the institution was held constant, the use of book theft systems resulted in lower losses. That is, comparing similar libraries with and without book theft systems shows that the systems do control losses.

Locked storage rooms were used by 53% of low crime libraries and 55% of the sample overall, but by an even higher proportion of high crime libraries (84%). Using a locked room for storage was more common in larger cities and in libraries with higher levels of AV and reference theft and vandalism inside the building.

Multiple Point Protection

Some types of security function to protect many areas of the library. This includes the use of security personnel and closed circuit television. There is, of course, some overlap here with specific point protection. However, a more general protection is appropriate when there are numerous risk areas or a generalized problem with crime.

Closed circuit television is an option that is rarely used in libraries. It does provide excellent general coverage of activities in many parts of the facility but is expensive to install, maintain and monitor. Less than 10% of the sample reported using the system. A similar proportion of high crime libraries had closed circuit TV in place. Use was related to the number of patrons and the circulation level but not to city size. In fact, almost all such systems were found in libraries with an annual circulation exceeding 500,000 items. Book theft and mutilation of materials was *lower* in libraries with closed circuit television.

The decision to use guards in the library usually is influenced by several factors, including the magnitude of the crime problem, the level of concern about personal safety and budget considerations. Keep in mind, however, that security personnel, while they reduce the crime problem, also change the atmosphere of the library setting. They are highly visible and serve as a constant reminder that the library is a place where problems occur. So there is both a deterrent effect and an image effect to be considered before deploying security personnel.

> Libraries in North London have had to be shut because of trouble from drunken vagrants and violent schoolchildren. In one case a man wielding a knife had to be disarmed by library staff, and a security guard was taken to hospital with broken ribs after an assault. . . . The libraries have had to close several times because staff refuse to work without proper security. . . . Meanwhile a dispute has broken out over the use of security guards at the libraries without the knowledge of councillors. (The Standard, London 11/1/84 p. 11)

> The branch had a previous very high record of break-ins—12 in 3 months. A security guard was installed for several months until renovations, including installation of a security system, were made.

Uniformed guards were employed by 12% of the libraries, but only 5% of the sample retained plainclothes security personnel. The figures were higher among high crime libraries, with 25% using uniformed guards and 15% employing plainclothes security. None of the low crime facilities retained any guards. Uniformed guards were more likely to be found in larger cities and in busier libraries. Twenty-five percent of the libraries in the largest cities but only 5%

of libraries in cities of under 100,000 had uniformed guards. There were none in the smaller city libraries. Plainclothes security personnel also were more likely to be used in libraries in larger cities. Several crime items were related to the use of uniformed guards, including reference theft, drug use and sales, indecent exposure and assault. In libraries without guards, 10% had more than 20 episodes of reference theft, compared with over 50% of libraries with guards. The use of plainclothes security was most closely associated with arson, drug use and sales, indecent exposure and theft.

Personnel Safety

> There have been problems with the harassment of staff by mainly groups of teenage hooligans. The problem was alleviated by employing extra staff to ensure that there were always two people working in the evenings.

There is probably no security issue that is more important than protecting personnel and patrons who work in and use the facility. While most security procedures already discussed contribute to this kind of protection, some specific precautionary measures can be taken. We asked about the use of four specific procedures that functioned primarily to protect staff and patrons. Some libraries (17%) had an escort system to assist staff in leaving the library. Almost 40% of the high crime libraries but none of the low crime libraries used an escort plan. In cities of over 100,000 more than a quarter of the libraries had staff escorts, while only 10% of the libraries in cities of under 100,000 used them. Circulation level and number of patrons were not related to the use of escorts. Vandalism outside the building, assault, arson and drug sales showed the strongest relationship to the use of escorts.

Staff training is another important ingredient in personnel safety. Relatively inexpensive programs can be arranged, using either police employees or private security specialists. In either case, the training can make employees more aware of potential problems and responses to these that will increase their own safety. Almost a third (30%) of the sampled libraries reported conducting training sessions (low crime = 0%; high crime = 57%). The sessions were most likely to be found in libraries in large cities with high levels of patron use. The level of verbal abuse of the staff and patrons was among the best predictors of staff training. Other crimes closely related to the use of staff training included reference theft, personal theft and interior vandalism.

> Teenagers coming in and shouting/pulling books off shelves are asked to leave by a male member of the staff. This has worked so far. Loss of some books and music tapes through theft has led to extra staff vigilance.

> We've worked on handling and cooling down potentially dangerous situations with patrons. A county wide training scheme is planned with other council departments.

One of the problems in protecting staff is the need for rapid communication by a staff member facing a crisis situation. Portable signalling devices were being used by the staff in 9% of the libraries studied. Communication links with police were used in 33% of the libraries overall and in 57% of high crime libraries. They were more common in libraries having more serious theft problems of various kinds than elsewhere. The use of portable signalling devices, while not common overall, was more likely to be found in libraries experiencing high levels of vandalism and personal theft. The signalling devices also were more common in libraries using security guards who could respond quickly to an alarm issued by a staff member.

Overall Security Use

Given the wide range of security options studied, what do we know about the likelihood of a library's having any type of security? The vast majority of the British central and district libraries, even low crime libraries, have some security in place. Half have more than 3 of the security items included in the survey. The overall level of security is positively correlated with high levels of book, reference, AV equipment and personal theft. However, we also found that assaults against staff were less likely to occur when the level of security was high. Several other crimes, including vandalism to cars, drug use and sales, arson and breaking and entering were no higher in the libraries with a great deal of security than in less secure libraries. This was true despite the fact that heavily secured libraries tended to be the larger, busier libraries in the larger cities. That is, security was effective in controlling the level of some of the crimes that would be anticipated in larger libraries.

National Differences in Security Patterns

It was shown in Chapter Two that highest overall levels of library crime were found in England, lower levels in Wales and lower still in Scotland. Examination of the overall use of security measures shows that this is highest in English libraries and lowest in Welsh libraries. However, somewhat different patterns emerge when the separate security items are examined as a function of location. For example, libraries in Wales were most likely to have security locks, smoke detectors and police patrol coverage. Scottish libraries were most likely to have locked storage rooms, intrusion alarms on doors and security screens. The remaining security items were most common among English libraries. In some cases, national differences were substantial. To illustrate, over 40% of Scottish libraries, 28% of English and 7% of Welsh had security screens. Patrol coverage was used by over a third of the libraries in Wales, 20% of the English and 12% of the Scottish.

SECURITY IN CANADIAN LIBRARIES

Property Line Protection

As was done in the study of British libraries, one question was asked about property line protection. Police patrol coverage was reported by 19% of the sample (see Table 5.2). Among the libraries reporting the highest incidence of crime, nearly half (48%) were using police patrols to help secure the facility and protect staff and patrons. Only 3% of low crime libraries reported using police patrols. In the entire sample, the larger the number of patrons using the library, the greater the likelihood of using police patrols. City size was inversely related to police patrol coverage. Smaller city libraries were more likely to use patrols than were libraries in larger cities. Libraries using patrol coverage were likely to have high levels of theft and vandalism, specifically book theft and other theft as well as vandalism outside the building.

> This is a small town where everyone knows everyone else. The biggest problem occurred when a man known to have convictions for molesting women began to make regular visits to the library. He began by staring at the young female staff and

Table 5.2

Proportion of Canadian Libraries Using Security Options

Type of Measure	Low Crime	High Crime	Total
Police patrol	3%	48%	18%
Security locks	20	72	42
Intrusion alarms (entry)	17	29	22
Security screens	8	23	18
Unbreakable windows	3	17	11
Intrusion alarms (interior)	6	29	14
Smoke/heat detector	19	84	38
Locked storage room	6	61	32
Book theft system	11	34	12
Surveillance cameras	0	0	2
Uniformed guards	3	10	5
Plainclothes guards	0	3	4
Escort for staff	0	31	10
Staff training	0	38	13
Portable alarms	3	7	4
Police communication link	3	26	12
Any of above items	39	100	73
Average number of crimes	0	107	30

later started to ask stupid questions about books. This caused great concern among the staff, and library regulations about what to do in such a case were very vague. We asked the police to increase their patrols and to watch out for him. The officer on patrol spoke to the man, and this seemed to have scared him off.

The most serious problem is broken windows—asked the police to keep a closer watch on the building.

Entry Point Protection

Several measures designed to improve the security of entry points were examined. Security locks were used by 42% of the Canadian public libraries. Of these, half had security locks on all entry doors and half had some doors secured in this way. Security locks on doors were more likely to be found in high crime libraries (34% had some, 38% had all) than in low crime libraries (9% had some, 11% had all). Security locks also were more likely to be found in libraries reporting high levels of vandalism outside the building, book and reference theft, arson and verbal abuse of the staff than in others.

Patrols deter crime both by their visibility and by the possibility of actually observing crimes in progress. Since not all illegal entry can be prevented by patrols, intrusion alarms are used in some libraries (22%). Close to half (44%) of high crime libraries and 17% of low crime libraries had at least some doors protected with intrusion alarms. Each entry door was equipped with an intrusion alarm in 28% of the high crime and 14% of the low crime libraries. The larger the city, the greater the number of patrons and the higher the circulation, the more likely that intrusion alarms were found on all doors. Several specific crimes tended to be higher in libraries that used intrusion alarms than in those that did not. These crimes included assault, vandalism inside the building and the various types of theft. Break-ins to the building were slightly lower among libraries with intrusion alarms.

> Break-ins to the building have occurred but are now solved by the installation of a burglar alarm.

While doors typically are the most common source of illegal entry, windows also are a preferred target for entry by intruders. Security screens were found in 18% of the libraries, and unbreakable windows were used by 11% of the sample. A smaller proportion had all windows secured with screens (9%) or with unbreakable glass (4%). High crime libraries were more than 5 times as likely as low crime libraries to use these measures. The use of security screens was associated with higher levels of equipment theft, vandalism and drug sales. Unbreakable windows were more likely to be found in libraries with high levels of vandalism inside the building and arson. There was a tendency for libraries with unbreakable windows to have lower levels of AV theft and other theft. Keep in mind that special provisions for escape from fire should be available when unbreakable windows/screens are being used.

> We have had some consistent window breakage after closing. We are attempting a replacement with plastic.

General Interior Protection

Two forms of general interior protection were investigated. The first, interior intrusion alarms, was used by 14% of the total sample but by 29% of the libraries in the high crime category. In contrast, only 6% of libraries with low levels of crime had intrusion alarms. Intrusion alarms were used more frequently in larger cities than in smaller places. For example, while 10% of the buildings in cities of less than 10,000 had such alarms, 30% of the libraries in cities of between 100-500,000 deployed intrusion alarms. Reference theft and equipment theft were positively related to the use of interior intrusion alarms, while arson was slightly lower when intrusion alarms were in place than when they were not.

Smoke and/or heat detectors were among the simpler security items included in the surveys. Over a third (39%) of the returns indicated that a detector was in place. More than 80% of the high crime libraries used smoke detectors, compared with 20% of the low crime libraries. Given the relatively low cost of these items, it is surprising that their use is not more widespread.

Specific Interior Protection

There is a marked contrast between the two interior protection items. The first, a locked storage room, is relatively inexpensive and serves to protect mostly noncirculating items. The second, book theft detection systems, is a costly addition to a library, and functions to protect both book and nonbook resources. Approximately a third of the Canadian sample used a locked storage room for protection. Once again, more high crime libraries (61%) than low crime libraries (6%) indicated that a secure storage room was used. Use was related to both city size and library size. Generally, as the reported level of theft increased, the likelihood of having a secure storage room also increased.

Book theft detection systems were found in 12% of the overall Canadian sample, and in 34% of the high crime libraries. About 10% of the libraries low in crimes had a book theft detection system. The larger the city and the higher the number of patrons served, the more likely a library was to have a system. To illustrate, only 6% of the libraries in towns of under 10,000, compared with 30% in cities of 100-500,000, used book theft systems. The highest rate of use was actually in cities of 50-100,000 (32%). Nearly half

(46%) of the libraries with book theft detection systems still reported more than 20 episodes of book theft annually. On the other hand, 18% of the libraries equipped with a book theft system did report that there were no known book thefts during the year. Considering that these were the larger, busier libraries, this compares favorably with the overall percentage of libraries reporting no book thefts (26%). Nearly a third (29%) of the libraries with book theft systems reported no theft of reference materials. There is some evidence that intentional book damage is higher in libraries with theft detection systems. For example, while only 12% of the libraries without the systems had more than 20 episodes of book mutilation, over a third of the libraries with the systems had 20 or more cases of mutilation during the year.

Multiple point protection.

> Undetected book theft is a problem—this problem is being looked at with respect to total stock security systems, closed circuit TV and mirrors.

As might be expected of security options that provide a wide range of protection, the expenses are high. The hiring of security guards, among the most costly security outlays, can provide a variety of protection services for major libraries. The guards may be employed directly by the library or may be under contract from a security service. Only 5% of Canadian libraries used uniformed security guards, while another 4% used plainclothes guards. In the high crime libraries uniformed guards were more likely to be found than plain clothes security personnel (uniformed = 10%, plainclothes = 3%). Both uniformed and nonuniformed security personnel were more likely to be found in large city libraries and when circulation and patron activity were high. While only 2 of 135 libraries in towns of under 2,500 had uniformed guards, such guards were found in 7 of 37 libraries in cities of 50-100,000 and 6 of 36 libraries in cities between 100-500,000. Surprisingly, none of the largest city libraries (over 500,000) reported having uniformed guards.

Similar patterns were found for nonuniformed guards. Their use peaked in cities of 50-100,000. Uniformed guards were most likely to be used in libraries with high levels of equipment theft and vandalism, indecent exposure, inside vandalism and drug sales. There was a tendency for arson, break-ins, and passing counterfeit money to be lower when guards were present, than when there were none. Nonuniformed guards were more common in libraries with high levels of other theft and drug sales. The presence of nonuniformed guards was associated with lower levels of book and reference theft, verbal abuse and vandalism outside the building. Both types of guards were found more often in libraries that had experienced higher than average institutional costs of crime, such as those associated with stopping programs for the community, changing hours as a result of crime and losing the use of equipment.

Only a small proportion of the sample (2%) reported using closed circuit television. As none of the 8 libraries with such a system was in the high crime category, indications are that the presence of the system did serve to control crime. This was true even though these libraries were in large cities and had high circulation and patron use. In fact, one major library with closed circuit television reported that it knew of no criminal acts during the year. Equipment theft was the only crime that tended to occur more often when closed circuit TV was used. However, given the small number of cases, these trends should be viewed cautiously.

Personnel Security

Four types of personnel security options were studied. Two of these, staff escorts and staff training, involved library policies, while the other two, the use of portable signalling devices and communication links, were hardware options. In 10% of cases, staff were escorted out of the building. This policy was in place in one-third of the high crime libraries, compared with none in the low crime libraries. Escorts were most common in libraries with high levels of theft, assault and problem patron behavior.

Staff training to manage crime and disruption was used in 14% of the libraries, and was more common in high crime (38%) than in low crime (0%) libraries. Training programs were related to high levels of assault, vandalism, theft and problem patron behavior.

> We have more than our share of disruptive teenagers during the winter months. We have talked to community and social workers with little effect. A county-wide training course recently held will hopefully produce guidelines for staff re-

sponses, but many feel that more staff are needed to keep the culprits occupied.

The behavior of school children during their holidays is our most serious concern. We are conducting staff training to control the problem.

Portable signalling devices were being used by only 4% of Canadian libraries. Use was slightly higher in high crime (7%) than in low crime (3%) libraries. The best predictors of the use of these devices were the rates of indecent exposure and theft. Automatic communication links with police were more common, being reported by 26% of high crime libraries, 3% of low crime libraries and 12% of the full sample. The links were most likely to be used in libraries with high levels of circulation and patron use. Small town libraries reported a 2% rate of use compared to a rate of about 25% in cities of between 10,000 and 500,000. The largest cities (over 500,000) had a lower rate of use (5%). Automatic communication links appeared more frequently in facilities with high levels of indecent exposure, verbal abuse to staff and vandalism inside the building.

Overall Security Patterns

Just over one quarter (27%) of the responding Canadian libraries had none of the security items asked about; 36% had only 1 or 2 of the options; and fewer than 10% had 6 or more. Among the high crime libraries, the patterns were different. All in this group had at least 2 of the items examined, and one quarter had at least 6. As expected, the low crime libraries were not free of crime because of heavy security, but rather had little security because the crime level to which they were subjected was low. Over 60% of these libraries made use of none of the security programs or items and nearly a quarter (23%) used only one.

The overall level of security was positively related to some of the variables studied, including several of the community characteristics and institutional factors. The strongest associations were with the level of patron use and city size. There was a tendency for more security to be deployed when the library was in an area designated as a lower socio-economic neighborhood than when it was elsewhere.

SECURITY IN UNITED STATES' LIBRARIES

The sampling of U.S. public libraries resulted in a library profile of relatively small libraries in small towns to medium-sized cities. In this sample then, the U.S. libraries resemble the Canadian libraries more than they do the British. The crime patterns described earlier also showed a greater similarity with Canadian libraries than with the busier British libraries. Since the same measures of security use were used in each study, it is possible to explore the same questions here as in the previous two sections of the chapter. What do the security patterns in the U.S. look like? What institutional, situational and crime factors relate to the type of security used or not used? These questions will be examined before we turn to a cross cultural comparison of security use in public libraries.

Property Line Protection

Police patrol coverage of the library was employed by 26% of the U.S. libraries. Figures for the security patterns in U.S. libraries are presented in Table 5.3. High crime libraries (34%) were more likely than low crime libraries (14%) to have patrol coverage. This average was more closely related to circulation level and number of patrons than it was to city size. The proportions of libraries with patrols ranged from 23% in the smallest cities and in cities of 100-500,000 to 31% in cities of 10-50,000. Patrols were more likely to be found in libraries with more than 50 patrons per day (28%) than in less active libraries (21%). Similarly, libraries circulating over 99,000 items per year used patrols more often (31%) than did libraries circulating fewer items. Libraries with high levels of verbal abuse to staff, vandalism to equipment and vandalism outside the building were particularly likely to use police patrols.

Entry Point Protection

A security lock was one of the most common types of security used. Nearly a quarter (22%) of the sample had some doors secured, while an additional 23% had all doors equipped with security locks. Only 19% of low crime libraries had any security locks on outside doors, compared with 65% of high crime libraries. The use of security locks was associated with higher levels of most of the different crime items. However, arson tended to be lower when security

Table 5.3

Proportion of U.S. Libraries Using Security Options

Type of Measure	Low Crime	High Crime	Total
Police patrol	14%	34%	26%
Security locks	19	65	46
Intrusion alarms (entry)	1	42	14
Security screens	5	17	12
Unbreakable windows	9	19	14
Intrusion alarms (interior)	2	27	12
Smoke/heat detector	13	59	27
Locked storage room	15	67	37
Book theft system	3	36	10
Surveillance cameras	0	3	1
Uniformed guards	1	13	5
Plainclothes guards	0	7	3
Escort for staff			17
Staff training			17
Portable alarms	0	9	4
Police communication link	4	24	12
Any of above items	41	97	76
Average number of crimes	0	105	29

locks were used. Break-ins were not assessed as part of the U.S. study. The relationship to city was clear. For each increase in the size of the city in which the library was located, there was a corresponding increase in the proportion of libraries using security locks. The same patterns held for increases in the number of patrons. The relationship between circulation level and the use of security locks was not as simple. Libraries with the lowest circulation levels (usually in very small towns and rural areas) were more likely than libraries with moderate circulation to have security locks, but the high circulation libraries were the most likely to use them.

Intrusion alarms were reported in 14% of the cases. Libraries with them were equally divided in terms of having some doors with alarms or all doors secured. High risk libraries used alarms more often (42%) than did low crime libraries (1%). Intrusion alarms were found more often in libraries in middle-sized cities, with high circulation and large numbers of patrons. Only 3 of 350 libraries serving fewer than 30 patrons per day had intrusion alarms on entry doors, compared with about a third of the libraries with over 100 patrons daily. High levels of equipment theft, vandalism to the inside of the building and to equipment and verbal abuse were good predictors of whether or not a library had intrusion alarms.

Window protection was not common among the libraries in the U.S. sample. Only 12% had any security screens; 7% with some windows secured in this way and 5% with all secured. A similar proportion (14%) used unbreakable windows. In roughly half of these cases, all windows were unbreakable. Security screens and unbreakable windows were most common in cities of 50-100,000 and least common in areas of less than 2,500. Increasing patron activity was directly related to the likelihood of using security screens, but unbreakable windows were equally likely to be found in libraries with low and middle levels of patron use. High patron use did correspond with greater use of security windows. The use of security screens and windows was comparable in all libraries except those with the highest circulation levels. The best predictor of using security windows was the level of vandalism outside the building. This is reasonable since unbreakable glass would be useful when the building itself is the target of vandals.

General Interior Protection

Despite the relatively low cost, only 27% of the surveys indicated that a smoke detector was in use. High crime libraries (59%) were nearly 5 times as likely as low crime libraries (13%) to use smoke detectors. Libraries in towns of under 2,500 had detectors in only 12% of cases, while city libraries (over 50,000) had a use rate of over 45%. Patron activity level and circulation both were positively associated with smoke detector use.

Interior intrusion alarms were used by 13% of the libraries in the study. Over a quarter of the highest crime libraries but only 1% of the lowest crime libraries had such a device. The highest use rates were in cities of 50-100,000 (30%) and cities of over 500,000 (27%), a strong contrast to use in towns of below 10,000 (5%). The number of patrons was a good predictor of use of intrusion alarms. The lowest rate was among libraries serving fewer than 50 patrons per day (3%) and the highest rate was in libraries with over 250 patrons daily (33%). Circulation patterns were related to intrusion alarm use in a similar fashion. The crimes most closely associated with use of intrusion alarms were reference theft, verbal abuse of the staff and vandalism outside the building.

> We have installed electronic security systems in all branches and the main library with exterior and interior detectors. In addition, we have installed everywhere fire detectors, which by the way failed to detect a serious fire in a branch that caused extensive damage. The detection systems seem to have prevented some loss from break-ins. They do, however, present numerous problems from false alarms and faulty equipment.

Specific Interior Protection

What proportion of U.S. libraries used a locked storage room for the protection of valuable items? Only 37% indicated that a room was available. Two thirds of the libraries faced with high crime and 15% of low crime libraries had a lockable storage room. A secured room was more typical of libraries in large cities (over 500,000 = 62%) than in small towns (under 10,000 = 26%). Generally a locked room was related to higher levels of circulation and patron activity. One of the best predictors of existence of a lockable room was the level of book and reference theft. As the levels of these crimes increased, the proportion of libraries using lockable rooms increased. The use of a locked room did appear to keep levels of equipment theft low. Considering that the larger and busier libraries were more likely to have locked rooms, it is significant that absence of theft of equipment in libraries with a locked room was about the same as in libraries without a lockable room.

The major theft problem faced by libraries is book theft. One in ten libraries reacted to this problem by using book theft detection systems. While just over 2% of low crime libraries had invested in theft detection systems, more than a third (36%) of the high risk libraries used a book theft system. Clearly, the systems were more common in large city libraries, being found in exactly one third of libraries in cities of over 100,000. A system was reportedly being used in only one library out of more than 400 in an area with fewer than 2,500 people. The level of patron activity was an even stronger predictor of having a system. Fewer than 3% of the libraries with under 100 patrons daily reported a system in use. Only 14% of libraries reporting between 100 and 250 patrons daily, but 41% of libraries with over 250 patrons, had operating book theft systems. Most of these busier libraries also circulated more than 100,000 pieces annually.

The use of this expensive but cost effective security option was closely related to having high levels of book damage, reference theft and verbal abuse to staff and patron. It appears that the level of book theft was being controlled. Ten percent of libraries with a theft system reported no known book thefts. An additional 27% indicated that fewer than 10 episodes of successful book theft were detected. However, there is some evidence that the level of mutilation is higher when book theft systems are in place. Nearly half (46%) of libraries with theft systems had at least 10 episodes of book damage. Only 13% of the libraries without theft systems had as much damage. This relationship was maintained when city size and activity level were held constant.

Multiple Point Protection

Neither uniformed nor nonuniformed guards were common in U.S. public libraries. In each case less than 5% of the sample reported that guards were used. A higher proportion of high crime libraries used uniformed guards (13%) and plainclothes guards (7%) than did low crime libraries (uniformed = 1%, nonuniformed = 0%). Both types of guards were most likely to be found in urban libraries. For example, 25% of libraries in cities of over 500,000 had uniformed guards, compared with 18% in cities of between 50-500,000 and fewer than 2% in cities under 50,000. Of the 107 libraries reportedly using some type of security guard, 96 were libraries serving over 100 patrons each day. The vast majority of these were libraries that circulated over 100,000 items annually. The levels of verbal abuse, indecent exposure and assault on patrons were strongly related to the likelihood of having guards. For example, while 5% of libraries without guards reported at least one assault on a patron, over 35% of those with a guard knew of an assault. Whether there would have been even more assaults in those libraries had they not hired a guard is a critical research question.

> We have had regular and productive meetings with members of the . . . Police Department, including the Chief of Police. The . . . Department has assigned one officer full time to the Central Library, and other officers "drop in" on a regular

basis to our branches. In addition we have a private security service which assists in monitoring. . . .

Closed circuit television was rare, reported by fewer than 2% of all libraries. Somewhat unexpectedly, the systems were found as often in cities of 10-50,000 as in the largest cities. Each of these libraries, regardless of city size, served large numbers of patrons and had high circulation. The closed circuit systems acted as good deterrents. Many of the crimes occurred no more often in these busy libraries with surveillance cameras than in less active libraries without systems. For example, while 32% of the full sample had no book damage, 26% of the libraries with TV also were free of damage. Equal proportions of libraries with and without TV were free of book theft and vandalism to equipment. None of the libraries with TV had any episodes of arson, compared with 4% of libraries without the systems.

Personnel Security

Two of the security options related to protection of personnel were equally likely to be reported. Programs providing for an escort of staff members to their cars were in place in 17% of the institutions. This was the same proportion that reported that staff training designed to deal with problems of crime and disruption was a part of the management plan of the library.

> We do many things: (1) Hourly department checks. (2) Eye control of all stairwells. (3) At least two people on a floor at one time. (4) All leave together at the same time, same exit in a group. All leave parking lot at the same time — no one is ever left alone on library grounds or in the building after dark.

Portable signalling devices were used rarely. Only 4% of the responses indicated that they were available. None of the low risk libraries and 9% of the high crime libraries reported having signalling devices. Again, we find that the proportion of libraries using the device increases as the size of the city increases. Fewer than 2% of libraries in areas below 10,000 and nearly 5% of mid-sized city libraries used signalling devices. In cities of more than a half million, 17% of libraries reported their use. There were less consistent relationships between patron activity and circulation level and use of portable signalling devices. High levels of patron assault, equipment and other theft and verbal abuse to staff were associated with using signalling devices. The correlation between having security personnel and using portable signalling devices was significant. This combination, of course, allows for rapid response to an incident in any area of the library.

Automatic communication links with police (12%) were more common than signalling devices (4%). Exactly one quarter of the high crime and 4% of low crime libraries were equipped with this option. Libraries in cities of 50-100,000 (23%) were the most likely to have the link-up, followed closely by the largest cities (21%). Generally, the greater the number of patrons using the library, the greater the likelihood of having communication with police. When there were more than 250 patrons daily, the proportion of libraries with the link-up was 28%. The proportion of libraries remained relatively constant (3-5%) until circulation reached 50,000 per year, and then jumped to 12%. The peak (24%) was reached among libraries circulating over 100,000 items. Libraries with communication links were characterized by relatively high levels of verbal abuse, reference theft, equipment vandalism and indecent exposure.

> Two staff people work together after dark for protection and have a link-up call with the sheriff's department.

Overall Security

Almost one quarter (24%) of U.S. libraries reported that they used none of the security items or programs described in the survey. An additional 36% had only 1 or 2 of the items. Five percent of the cases had at least 8 different security options. While it is not surprising that 59% of low risk libraries had no security program, it is alarming that 13% of high risk libraries used no security measures or only one. Half of the high crime cases had 5 or more items. The level of security was influenced by several factors. There was more security in libraries in bigger cities, with higher patron use levels and with greater circulation. The best predictor of these three was the size of the city. Also, when the perceived effect of crime on service to the public was high, the overall level of security was high. Finally, high levels of security were associated with frequent book theft, mutilation and verbal abuse of staff.

Regional Differences

Earlier in this work it was shown that crime in the United States varied from region to region. Generally, the western states had the highest crime rates, but there were exceptions for specific types of crime. Do responses to crime in the nation's libraries show regional patterns? That is, is the use of security more common in one region than another? In some instances the differences are substantial. For example, libraries in the Northeast were more than twice as likely as those in any other region to have electronic intrusion alarms, communication links with police, plainclothes security and unbreakable windows. On the other hand, these libraries were the least likely to have police patrol coverage and security locks. Libraries in the southern states were the most likely to have security locks and a locked storage room. Western libraries used police patrols more frequently than others, but were least likely to have security personnel and unbreakable windows. Overall, more libraries in the north central region had none of the security devices or programs. Northeastern and southern libraries were about equally likely (80%) to have at least one security option. The average number of security options in place in northeastern libraries was 2.9, compared with 2.5 in southern and 2.2 in both north central and western facilities.

Effect of Security

The studies conducted in Canada and the United States assessed the effect of security on the level of crime. This was measured by asking: "If you installed security devices or hired security personnel within the last three years, then how much has crime and disruption declined?" What does this tell us? First of all, it provides an indication of the proportion of libraries that did install security or implement some crime reduction program within the previous three years. Secondly, information is made available on how effective the program was in reducing crime. What is not determined by the question is what kind of security is being referred to. Since many libraries had several different devices in place, any decline could have resulted from a combination of security factors or changes in the community that affected crime levels. However, some information on the effectiveness of security can be obtained.

The U.S. study found that approximately 30% of the sample had taken some security measures within the previous three years. Of the libraries in this group, 74% indicated that crime and disruption had not declined since the security item was added. Twelve percent indicated that crime declined by 50% or less, and 15% indicated that crime was cut by more than 50%. In fact, 6% of libraries installing security items told of crime reductions of 90%. Libraries that had book theft systems were more likely to report large declines in crime problems.

Similar patterns were found in Canada. Nearly a quarter (23%) of the respondents told of adding security items within a three year period. Of those libraries, 65% found no decrease in crime and disruption. Crime was cut by between 10% and 50% in a quarter of the libraries. Seven percent of the sample had estimated crime reductions of 90%. The crimes that appeared to have declined most noticeably when respondents indicated significant reductions following security deployment were book theft, assault and drug use. This is consistent with the finding that libraries with book theft systems and security personnel reported relatively high levels of crime reduction. Even the Canadian libraries falling into the high crime category (those with crime rates at the top 10% of the scale) showed crime decline when security was added. At the same time, equal proportions of these libraries reported no decline and declines of 50% or more following security installation. The larger declines were more common in libraries with book theft systems.

COMPARATIVE SECURITY PATTERNS

Are libraries in any one nation more likely to have security programs than libraries in other countries? Ideally, the answer to this question should take into account the differences between the community and institutional characteristics of the libraries in the different locations. As was done in the comparisons of crime patterns, similar types of libraries should be studied when doing cross-cultural comparisons. The libraries in Canada and the United States indeed are similar, while the sampled British libraries are somewhat larger and busier. We also have seen that these particular British libraries tended to have higher crime rates than libraries in the other samples. Do they also have more security? Generally they are more secure. Only 8% of the British sample had none of the measured security items. In contrast, approximately one quarter of the U.S.

and Canadian libraries were without any security. (See Table 5.4.)

However, the British libraries were not the most likely to have each of the security items in question. Police patrols were most common in the U.S. libraries (26%) and less common in the British (20%) and Canadian (18%) libraries. Smoke and heat detectors were found most often in the Canadian libraries (38%), followed by the U.S. (27%) and British (26%) libraries. The use of security locks was similar in the three samples. The remaining items were used most frequently by the libraries in Great Britain.

Since the U.S. and Canadian libraries are similar, it is possible to compare them in more detail. There were similar deployment patterns for security locks, unbreakable windows, intrusion alarms, book theft systems, surveillance cameras, guards, portable alarms and communication links with police. Libraries in the U.S. were more likely to have police patrols, locked storage rooms, and staff

Table 5.4

Proportion of Libraries Using Security Options

Type of Measure	U.S.A.	Canada	G.B.
Police patrol	26%	18%	20%
Security locks	46	42	44
Intrusion alarms (entry)	14	22	36
Security screens	12	18	24
Unbreakable windows	14	11	34
Intrusion alarms (interior)	12	14	36
Smoke/heat detector	27	38	26
Locked storage room	37	32	55
Book theft system	10	12	26
Surveillance cameras	1	2	8
Uniformed guards	5	5	12
Plainclothes guards	3	4	5
Escort for staff	17	10	17
Staff training	17	13	30
Portable alarms	4	4	8
Police communication link	12	12	33
Any of above items	76	73	92
Average number of crimes	29	30	69

The U.S. and Canadian samples are representative.
The British sample includes central and district libraries.

escorts and training programs. The Canadian libraries were more likely to have entrance intrusion alarms, security screens and smoke detectors. The proportions of libraries having at least one of the devices or programs were nearly identical.

If libraries from comparably sized cities are examined, then the differences between the U.S./Canadian and British libraries diminish but do not disappear. The scarcity of small town libraries in the British sample keep the security use figures high. For example, British libraries overall were more than twice as likely to have book theft systems, but in cities of 100-500,000 the systems were found in 32% of U.S. libraries, 30% of Canadian and 41% of British. Similarly, in smaller cities (10-50,000) book theft systems were being used in 17% of U.S. libraries, 11% of Canadian and 15% of British.

In some cases, the use of security is similar for libraries of the different countries for one city size but not for others. For example, automatic communication links with police were used by 24% of British and Canadian libraries in cities of 10-50,000 and by 20% of comparable U.S. libraries. In larger cities of 100-500,000, the U.S. and Canadian rates remained the same, but the British use rose to 41%. Similarly, in cities of 50-100,000 uniformed security guards were more common in Canadian (19%) and U.S. (18%) libraries than in British (6%) libraries. However, in larger city libraries, only 10% of Canadian compared to 21% of U.S. and British libraries used uniformed guards. It appears that the decisions to implement security options are based on similar factors in each of the nations studied. The level of crime in the library, the size of the city and the magnitude of crime in the community, the activity level of the library and the library budget influence the type and amount of security found in the library.

SUMMARY

Sixteen security options were studied. These included various types of property line protection, entry point protection, interior protection and personnel safety programs. Property line protection is the "first line of defense" for the library.

Police patrols were used by 20% of British libraries, and were more common when the levels of equipment theft, vandalism, assault and break-ins were high.

There is both a deterrent effect and an image effect to consider before deploying security personnel.

One of the problems in protecting staff is the need for rapid communication by a staff member facing a crisis situation.

Among the libraries in Great Britain, security steps were more likely to be implemented by English libraries and least likely in Scottish libraries, but there were differences depending upon the type of security item in question. Police patrols were found more often in Canadian libraries with high levels of verbal abuse to staff and vandalism.

In Canadian libraries the use of expensive but cost effective security options was related to high levels of book damage, reference theft and verbal abuse.

There is some evidence that the level of book damage is higher when book theft systems are in place.

Security locks, locked storage rooms, smoke detectors and police patrols were the most common types of security options used by U.S. libraries.

Approximately one fourth of U.S. and Canadian libraries reported using none of the security options studied. Over 90% of the British sample had at least one of the items.

The use of book theft systems was related to city size. For example, in large cities the systems were found in 41% of British, 32% of U.S. and 30% of Canadian libraries. In cities of 10-50,000, they were used by 15% of British, 17% of U.S. and 11% of Canadian libraries.

Libraries in the British sample overall were more likely than those in the U.S. and Canadian samples to use security measures. Slight differences remained even when city size was controlled.

Libraries reporting high levels of crime generally were more likely than others to report having higher levels of security.

REFERENCES

Lincoln, Alan J., *Crime in the Library: A Study of Patterns, Impact and Security*, (New York: R. R. Bowker, 1984).

Lincoln, Alan J. and Lincoln, Carol Z., "The impact of crime in public libraries," *Library and Archival Security*, 3, (1980):125-137.

Chapter Six

Controlling Crime: A Security Checklist

A great deal of information about crime and its effects have been presented in previous chapters. Several general conclusions can be drawn from the three studies. It is clear that crime is common in libraries in all of the countries studied. Furthermore, the range of crime problems is substantial. While some libraries suffer only minor problems of book theft, many others experience property crimes as well as crimes against persons. It also has been shown that community and institutional factors affect the patterns of crime. Since security programs are designed to deal with actual and anticipated problems, it stands to reason that these programs will vary from location to location. Yet it is possible to suggest some precautions and measures that may be useful to libraries facing a wide range of problems.

> The Ann Arbor Public Library has adopted new rules for patrons that bar the sleepy and the extremely smelly, and a civil liberties group is worried that the result will be discrimination against "street people." The rules are among 30 guidelines, approved last week, which, among other things, prohibit fighting, drugs, weapons, gambling and alcoholic beverages in the city's libraries. . . . (Associated Press, 11/22/84)

> A drifter who held a grudge against women bought a revolver less than two hours before he walked into the public library and opened fire, killing a library worker and wounding two other women, one of them critically, police said. (Associated Press, 12/20/84)

In this final chapter, we will begin with an overview of several issues related to protecting the library and follow this with a model security checklist that can be modified to meet local needs. Many of the options included in this list are related to the risk factors described in Chapter One. At that time, we suggested that public libraries were at risk because of valued contents, ease of access, unusual schedule, public attitudes and so on. Any attempts to reduce the level of crime should keep in mind the desired atmosphere of the library. While it is possible to secure a public building, even a high risk facility, the effort may alter the preferred environment to such an extent that the goals and mission of the institution are compromised. The security checklist emphasizes alternatives that will help to maintain a safe and secure facility without dramatically altering the library setting. An attempt also has been made to identify security options that are relatively low in cost.

The problem of security and crime prevention is multifaceted. There are many ways to approach this problem. In Chapter Five the general examination of security used by the sampled libraries included property line and entry point protection, specific and general interior protection, multiple point security and personnel safety. In organizing an overview of security requirements, many factors have to be taken into account. Regardless of which organizational scheme is adopted, it must be recognized that crime prevention is a complex issue and that total "success" is unlikely. The better security programs address a variety of actual and potential threats. This complexity is acknowledged by Bottom and Kostanoski (1983) in their volume on loss control:

> *Security and Loss Control* addresses the "whys" of security as well as the problems of loss. It makes a concession to the futility of loss prevention by taking the position of loss control. It introduces a new way of looking at an old and persistent problem. The traditional crime orientation of security is replaced with a multiloss orientation. Loss control includes waste, accident, error, crime, and unethical practice (WAECUP). It perceives of loss as a constant; thus loss acceptance is one of its philosophical cornerstones. Loss control maintains that WAECUP threats are interrelated both in cause and effect—that error, for example, can be an interrelated cause of crime and that toleration of waste may lead to accident. (p. ix)

Similarly, Gallery's introduction to *Physical Security* (1986) suggests that:

Effective security depends upon the skillful integration of security policies and procedures, personnel, and physical security measures. Physical security measures are often thought of solely in terms of hardware, but may encompass design factors as well. . . . By itself hardware is seldom the full solution to the problem of protecting assets. It is, however, often a valuable component in the security program, provided the selected hardware relates logically to the other facets of the program. . . . Without adequate procedural and personnel support, physical security measures will almost invariably fall short of expectations. (p. xi)

We have already described the use patterns of many of the options available to protect the facility and personnel. These included various property line protection, entry point protection and interior protection devices. For the reader seeking more information, several recent detailed accounts are available of ways to protect the library facility and contents, including work by Bahr (1981, 1984) on electronic security for books; and by Boss (1984), Crimmin (1984), Brawner and Nelson (1984), Brand (1984) and Lincoln (1984) on more general protection programs for libraries.

Also available are a number of recent library crime and security bibliographies that are useful to administrators and staff concerned about these problems. Among the more comprehensive listings are those by Gandert (1982), Sable (1983), Brawner and Nelson (1984) and Wicker (1984). While the security checklist that follows is extensive, it certainly is not exhaustive. Issues not addressed here can be added as their need becomes apparent.

SECURITY CHECKLIST

1. Property line protection:

   —Eliminate/avoid hidden locations outside building
   —Provide adequate visibility in parking areas
   —Do not conceal windows/doors from view
   —Trim shrubs so they do not block visibility
   —Adjust fences so they do not block visibility
   —Provide low-profile landscaping around exterior
   —Keep the exterior well lit

- Use vandal-proof lighting
- Use night light timers/electric eyes
- Do not use throwable rocks in landscaping
- Arrange for police patrol on an unpredictable basis
- Have police patrols at critical times

2. Entry point control:

- Door locks that are difficult to pick or damage
- Deadbolt or sequential combination pushbutton locks
- Door hinges should be on inside
- Reinforce any exposed hinges
- Breakresistant materials in door glass
- Reinforce door frames
- Secure roll-down doors
- Install a sequence lock system
- Entry monitoring system
- Entry points should have adequate alarms
- Patrons should not enter/exit undetected
- Use turnstyles to slow and control exiting
- Use exit attendants
- Windows should have security locks
- Security screens on windows
- Break resistant windows
- Airconditioners should be secured from inside
- Keys should be marked "Do not duplicate"
- Multilevel master key system
- Lock exchanges to maintain integrity of system
- Develop a "lock-up" procedure
- Fire escape should be secured
- Fire escape alarm to indicate use
- Vents and ducts should be secured
- Skylights should be secured
- Consider a monitoring contract
- Improve control of emergency exits

3. Interior space control:

- Posters and displays should not block vision
- Avoid or eliminate hidden areas in building
- Arrange stacks for maximum visibility

— Place "peepholes" in book stacks
— Have visibility of study areas
— Consider mirrors to improve visibility
— Closed circuit TV/"dummy" cameras
— Provide adequate interior lighting
— Do not let people "hang out" in risk areas
— Silent alarms/panic buttons in bathrooms
— Limit access to bathrooms
— Control access to elevators
— Protect partition walls that can be climbed
— Keep staff areas locked

4. Management of materials and contents:

— Smoke and fire alarms
— Evaluate insurance coverage
— Minimize cash in building
— Remove cash frequently using secure procedure
— Reduce staff and patron access to cash
— Provide secure storage for cash
— Maintain record of all cash transactions
— Provide receipts/encourage asking for such
— Cash transactions in visible area
— Library policies written and available
— Consistent application of policies
— Book/materials theft system
— Check inventories often enough to notice theft
— Participate in theft clearinghouse
— Closed stacks for valuable items
— Reserved stacks for items in demand
— Learn names of patrons
— Limit carrying by patrons of bags and parcels
— Utilize staff inspection
— Post notice of laws and penalties for book theft
— Publicize theft problem and its cost
— Keep back issues of periodicals on microfilm
— Properly mark library materials
— Have reasonable loan and renewal policies
— Have adequate parking to encourage returns
— Fireproof receptacle for returns
— Close book drop if being misused

- Double check machine-readable transactions
- Arrange for periodic renewal of cards
- Simple registration procedures for new user
- Quick and efficient checkout
- Few restrictions on number of items checked
- Reserve system for demand items
- Overnight circulation of reserves
- Reference circulation on limited basis
- Multiple copies of high demand items
- No fine policy/low fine policy
- Bonuses for no overdues and returns
- Provide secure book drop off for after hours
- Amnesty days
- Monitor reserve rooms
- Staff circulating on floors
- Deposits on selected checkouts
- Mailgrams or collectors for overdues
- Identify rare materials
- Alarms for areas housing rare materials
- Restrict staff/patron access to rare materials
- Maintain current inventory of rare items
- Charge actual value for "lost" rare items
- Post penalties for mutilation
- Publicize problem by displaying mutilated material
- Access to low cost photocopy
- Be sure that change is available
- Provide "free" copy card as part of fees
- Repair/remove mutilated materials
- Procedure to assess damage after use
- Coordinate assignments with public schools
- "Give away" file
- Use vandal resistant materials
- Keep valuables in a locked area
- Keep desks locked
- Keep staff belongings in locked area
- Publicize problem of theft
- Publicize apprehension of thieves
- Post signs alerting users to problems
- Provide lockers for staff/patrons
- Secure equipment to work stations
- Keep equipment in supervised or locked areas

— Remove portable equipment from public areas
— Pressure sensitive alarms for equipment
— Engrave library ID on equipment
— Publicize that equipment is marked
— Keep current inventory of equipment
— Arrange displays to notice missing items
— Use security alarms on displays
— Use pressure sensitive pads
— Keep cases in public view
— Secure base of cases from access
— Locate vending machines in visible area
— Empty machines each night and post notice
— Alarms on machines and post notice
— Use tokens/cards for photocopying
— Limit access to computers
— Copy disks and secure outside library
— Computer room always staffed or locked
— Fire protection for computer area
— Limit issuing of password/access control
— Audit trails for record changes

5. Protecting personnel:

— Develop procedure for reporting crime
— Train staff in crime prevention
— Have evacuation plans for fire, bomb threats
— Have panic buttons
— Have portable communication links
— Use security guards (inhouse or contract)
— Staff ID badges
— Emergency telephones
— Develop secret codes for emergencies
— Avoid having employees work alone
— Staff escorts out of building
— Access to legal counsel

6. Protection from Personnel:

— Develop procedure for reporting employee crime
— Do not ignore minor crime and theft
— Develop guidelines for prosecution of employees

— Prosecute when necessary
— Conduct background and reference checks
— Clearly state policies concerning employee behavior
— Do not ignore minor employee infractions
— Record use of vital records
— Limit access to personnel records
— Limit access to computers
— Issue keys on need basis
— Recover ID cards upon termination
— Visual control of employee exits
— Limit access to telephone
— Limit access to cash and supplies
— Colorcode badges by access level
— Library vehicle security and access policy

REFERENCES

Bahr, Alice H., *Book Theft and Library Security Systems*, (White Plains, New York: Knowledge Industry Publications, 1981).
Bahr, Alice H., "Electronic security for books," *Library and Archival Security*, 3, (1984):29-38.
Boss, Richard W., "Collection security," *Library and Archival Security*, 3, (1984): 39-48.
Bottom, Norman R. and Kostanoski, John, *Security and Loss Control*, (New York: Macmillan Publishing Company, 1983).
Brand, Marvine, *Security for Libraries: People, Buildings, Collections*, (Chicago: ALA, 1984).
Brawner, Lee B., and Nelson, Norman, "Improving security and safety for libraries," *Public Library Quarterly*, 5, (1984): 41-58.
Crimmin, Wilbur B., "Institutional, personal, collection, and building security concerns," in M. Brand, *Security for Libraries*, (Chicago: ALA, 1984).
Gallery, Shari M., *Physical Security*, (Boston: Butterworth Publishers, 1986).
Gandert, Slade R., *Protecting Your Collection*, (New York: Haworth Press, 1982).
Lincoln, Alan J., *Crime in the Library: A Study of Patterns, Impact and Security*, (New York: R. R. Bowker, 1984).
Lincoln, Alan J. and Lincoln, Carol Z., "The impact of crime in public libraries," *Library and Archival Security*, 3, (1980):125-137.
Sable, Martin H., *The Protection of the Library and Archive: An International Bibliography*, (New York: Haworth Press, 1983).
Wicker, William W., "Selected readings on library security," in M. Brand, *Security for Libraries*, (Chicago: ALA, 1984).

Bibliography

Bahr, Alice H., *Book Theft and Library Security Systems* (White Plains, New York: Knowledge Industry Publications, 1981).

Bahr, Alice H., "Electronic security for books," *Library Trends* 3 (1984): 29-38.

Boss, Richard W., "Collection security," *Library Trends* 3 (1984): 39-48.

Bottom, Norman R. and Kostanoski, John, *Security and Loss Control* (New York: Macmillan Publishing Company, 1983).

Brand, Marvine, *Security for Libraries: People, Buildings, Collections* (Chicago: ALA, 1984).

Brawner, Lee B., and Nelson, Norman, "Improving security and safety for libraries," *Public Library Quarterly*, 5 (1984): 41-58.

Camp, John F., "Security systems," in American Library Association Yearbook (Chicago: ALA, 1985), pp. 258-259.

Canada Yearbook, Ministry of Industry, Trade and Commerce (Quebec: 1978).

Crimmin, Wilbur B., "Institutional, personal, collection, and building security concerns," in M. Brand, 1984.

Encyclopedia of Library and Information Science (New York: Marcel Dekker, Inc., 1976).

Gallery, Shari M., *Physical Security* (Boston: Butterworth Publishers, 1986).

Gallup, George, The Gallup Poll., June 7, 1979; March 8, 1981 (Princeton, N.J.).

Gates, Jean K., *Introduction to Librarianship* (New York: McGraw Hill, 1968).

Gendert, Slade R., *Protecting Your Collection* (New York: The Haworth Press, 1982).

Hookway, H.T., "The British library," in W.L. Saunders (Ed.) British Librarianship Today (London: The Library Association, 1976) pp. 37-45.

Hoppe, Ronald and Simmel, Edward, "Book tearing and the bystander in the university library," *College and Research Libraries*, 30 (1969):247-251.

Lincoln, Alan J., *Crime in the Library: A Study of Patterns, Impact and Security* (New York: R. R. Bowker, 1984).

Lincoln, Alan Jay, "Patterns and costs of crime," *Library Trends*, 33:1 (1984):69:76.

Lincoln, Alan J. and Lincoln, Carol Z., "The impact of crime in public libraries," *Library & Archival Security*, 3 (1980):125-137.

Parker, Peter, "Statutory protection of library materials," *Library Trends*, 33 (1984):77-94.

Phillips, B.J., "Public libraries: Legislation, administration and finance" (London: The Library Association, 1977).

Predeek, Albert, *A History of Libraries in Great Britain and North America* (Chicago: ALA, 1947).

Research and Forecasts Inc., *The Figgie Report on Fear and Crime: American Afraid* (Willoughby, Ohio: A.T.O., Inc), 1980.

Sable, Martin H., *The Protection of the Library and Archive: An International Bibliography* (New York: The Haworth Press, 1983).

Stewart, Linda, "Never mind the answer, what's the question?" (Loughborough, England: Centre for Library and Information Management, 1984).

United States Department of Justice, *Report to the Nation on Crime and Justice* (Washington, DC), 1983.

Wicker, William W., "Selected readings on library security," in M. Brand, *Security for Libraries* (Chicago: ALA, 1984).

Wilson, Alexander, "Public libraries," in W.L. Saunders (Ed.) *British Librarianship Today* (London: The Library Association, 1976), pp. 170-203.

Index

Access, as library crime risk factor, 12-13
Activity level, as library crime correlate, 14
  in British libraries, 42-45
  in Canadian libraries, 72-73
  in United States libraries, 103-104
Alarm systems. *See also* Signalling devices
  in British libraries, 118-119,120,125
  in Canadian libraries, 126,127,128
  comparative patterns of use, 141
  in United States libraries, 133,134-135, 139
American Library Association
  founding of, 10
  "Minimum Standards for Public Library Systems," 11
Arson
  in British libraries, 28,31,32,44,45,46, 49,50,53,54,56,120
  in Canadian libraries, 65,66,73,76,77, 80,82
  in United States libraries, 97,98-99, 103-104,105,106,107
Assault
  on patrons
    in British libraries, 28,31,40,44,46, 47
    in Canadian libraries, 65,66,70,72, 73,76,78,80,81
    in United States libraries, 97,102, 104,106,107
  prevention, 3
  on staff
    in British libraries, 28,31,40-41,44, 45,46,47,48,49,50
    in Canadian libraries, 65,66,67,73, 76,77-78,80
    in United States libraries, 90,92, 97,102,103-104,105,106,107

Audio alarms, 119
Audio-visual material, theft of
  in British libraries, 28,31,34,35,44,45, 46
  in Canadian libraries, 65,66,67,73,76, 77-78,80
  in United States libraries, 107

Billing, fraudulent
  in British libraries, 28,31,35,44,46,47
  in Canadian libraries, 65,66,68,73,76, 77,80,82
  in United States libraries, 107
Bodley, Thomas, 5
Books
  intentional damage
    in British libraries, 28,29-30,31,43, 44,46
    in Canadian libraries, 64,65,66,72, 73,74,76,79,80,81,82,86
    in United States libraries, 96-97,103, 104,105,106,107,108
  theft
    in British libraries, 28,31,33-35, 43-44,46,48,49,50
    in Canadian libraries, 65,66,67-68, 72,73,74,76,77,79,80,81,82,87
    in United States libraries, 97,99,103, 104,106,107
  theft protection systems
    in British libraries, 120-121
    in Canadian libraries, 126,128-129
    comparative patterns, 141,142
    in United States libraries, 133, 135-136
Boston Public Library, 10
Bourdillon Report, 6

155

Breaking and entering. *See also* Entry
  point protection; Property line
  protection
 in British libraries, 28,31,36,44,46,
  47,49,50,53,54,55
 in Canadian libraries, 65,66,68-69,73,
  76,77,80,82,85
 in United States libraries, 97,107
British Library Act of 1972, 6-7
Building design, as library crime risk
  factor, 14
Burglary, 20,22,23,92

Cambridge University, 5
Camera surveillance. *See* Closed circuit
  television
Canada
 crime offenders' characteristics, 61-62
 crime patterns, 90,91-92,93
 crime rates, 59-61,62
  city size correlation, 61,62
  provincial differences, 61
 library crime, 59-88
  assault, 65,66,70,72,73,76,78,79,
   80,81,86
  community factors, 74-82
  costs, 82-87
  institutional factors, 72-74
  patterns, 64-71
  personal victimization, 71
  provincial differences, 75-79
  theft, 65,66,67-69,73,76,77,78,79,
   80,81,82,84,85,86,87
  vandalism, 64-71,72-73,74,77,79,
   80,81,82,84,85,86
 library security, 125-131,140,141,
   142,143
  crime effects, 140
  entry point protection, 126-127
  general interior protection, 128
  multiple point protection, 129-130
  overall patterns, 131
  personnel security, 126,130-131
  specific interior protection, 128-129
 public library development, 7-9
Canadian Library Association, 8
Canadian Urban Victimization Study, 60
Carnegie, Andrew, 11

Carnegie United Kingdom Trust, 6
Carnegie-supported libraries, 6,8
Cars, vandalism to
 outside British libraries, 28,31,32,44,
  45,46,47,49,50
 outside Canadian libraries, 65,66,73,
  76,77,79,80,82
 outside United States libraries, 97,98,
  104,106,107
City size
 as crime correlate
  in Canada, 61-62
  in United States, 91-92
 as library crime correlate
  in British libraries, 45-47,121-123
  in Canadian libraries, 72-73,74-75,
   76,77,79-81
  closed circuit television and, 122
  in United States, 103,105-107
Closed circuit television
 in British libraries, 121-123
 in Canadian libraries, 126,130
 comparative patterns, 141
 in United States libraries, 137
Closing, of library, as crime response
 by British libraries, 53
 by Canadian libraries, 84,87
 by United States libraries, 110
Communication, with police
 by British libraries, 123,141
 by Canadian libraries, 141
 comparative patterns, 141
 by United States libraries, 133,138,
  139,141
Community factors, as library crime
  correlate
 in British libraries, 47-50
 in Canadian libraries, 74-82,85,87
 in United States libraries, 105-108
Community program discontinuation, as
  crime response
 by British libraries, 53,54
 by Canadian libraries, 85
 by United States libraries, 110,111
Counterfeit money use
 in British libraries, 28,31,35-36,44,
  46,47,49,50
 in Canadian libraries, 65,66,68,73,
  76,77,79,80,82

Index

in United States libraries, 97
Crime. *See also* Crime, library
 in Canada, 90,91-92,93
  rate, 59-61,62
  trends, 59-61
 categorization, 26-27
 cross-cultural similarities, 19
 factors related to, 2-3
 in Great Britain
  offenders' characteristics, 22-23
  patterns, 19-23,90,91,92,93
  rate, 20-23
  trends, 21-23
 increasing rate, 2-3
 public attitudes towards, 16,20,89
 in United States
  city size correlation, 91-92
  patterns, 89-94
  rate, 90-93
  regional variations, 92-93
Crime, library
 in British libraries, 19-58
  assault, 28,31,40-41,44,45,46,47
  community factors, 47-50
  costs, 50-57
  institutional factors, 42-47
  patron problem behavior, 37-40
  patterns, 26-41
  personal victimization, 41-42
  theft, 28,31,33-37,43-44,46,48,49,
   50,53,54
  vandalism, 28,29-32,44-45,46,53,
   54,55
 in Canadian libraries, 59-88
  assault, 65,66,70,72,73,76,78,79,
   80,81,86
  community factors, 74-82
  costs, 82-87
  institutional factors, 72-74
  patterns, 64-71
  personal victimization, 71
  provincial differences, 75-79
  theft, 65,66,67-69,73,76,77-78,
   79,80,81,82,84,85,86,87
  vandalism, 64-67,72-73,74,77,79,
   80,81,82,84,85,86
 costs
  in British libraries, 50-57
  in Canadian libraries, 82-87

in United States libraries, 108-113
risk factors, 12-17
 activity level, 14,42-45
 building design, 14
 desirable contents, 13
 ease of access, 12-13
 lack of crime prevention training,
  13-14
 lack of security, 13
 legislation and, 14-16
 librarians' attitudes, 16
 patrons' age, 13,73-74
 public attitudes, 16
 schedule, 13
security effects, 139-140
in United States libraries, 94-113
 community factors, 105-108
 comparative analysis, 96-113
 costs, 108-113
 institutional factors, 103-105
 problem patron behavior, 100-103
 theft, 97,99-100
 vandalism, 96-99,104,105,107,108
Crime Index, 89
Crime prevention
 costs
  in British libraries, 51-52
  in Canadian libraries, 83,84
  in United States libraries, 109-110
 staff training, 13-14
  in British libraries, 56-57,123-124
  in Canadian libraries, 126,130-131
  comparative patterns, 141
  in United States libraries, 110
Crime statistics
 underestimation, 27-28
 Uniform Crime Reports, 89-94
 unreliability of, 20-21
Criminals. *See* Offenders

Drug sales/use
 in British libraries, 28,31,37,38,44,46,
  47,49,50,53,54
 in Canadian libraries, 65,66,69,73,76,
  79,80
 in United States libraries, 97,100-101,
  104,106,107

England. *See* Great Britain
Entry point protection
 in British libraries, 118-119
 in Canadian libraries, 126-127
 security checklist, 148
 in United States libraries, 132-134
Equipment
 damage
  in British libraries, 31-32,44,46,49, 50
  in Canadian libraries, 65,66,73,74, 76,77,80,85
  in United States libraries, 97,98,104, 106,107
 loss of use
  in British libraries, 53,54
  in Canadian libraries, 85,87
  in United States libraries, 110
 theft
  in British libraries, 28,31,35,44,46, 47,49,50
  in Canadian libraries, 65,66,68,73, 76,77,80,85,86
  in United States libraries, 97,99-100, 104,106
Escort service, for staff
 in British libraries, 122
 in Canadian libraries, 126,130
 comparative patterns, 141
 in United States libraries, 110,133,137

Forced entry. *See* Breaking and entry
Franklin, Benjamin, 10
Fraud/forgery, in Great Britain, 20,22

Great Britain. *See also* Scotland; Wales
 crime
  offenders' characteristics, 22-23
  patterns, 19-23,90,91,92,93
  rate, 20-23
  trends, 21-23
 library crime, 19-58
  assault, 28,31,40-41,44,45,46,47
  community factors, 47-50
  costs, 50-57
  institutional factors, 42-47

  patron problem behavior, 37-40
  patterns, 26-41
  personal victimization, 41-42
  theft, 28,31,33-37,43-44,46,48,49, 50,53,54
  vandalism, 28,29-32,44-45,46,53, 54,55
 library security, 114-125,140,142,143
  entry point protection, 118-119
  general interior protection, 119-120
  multiple point protection, 121-123
  overall use patterns, 124
  property line protection, 116-118
  specific interior protection, 120-121
 public library development 5-7
Guards. *See* Security personnel

Harassment. *See* Verbal abuse
Heat detectors
 in British libraries, 120
 in Canadian libraries, 126,128
 comparative patterns, 141
 in United States libraries, 133
Homicide, handguns and, 21-22
Homicide rate
 in Canada, 21,59,60,61,62,90
 in Great Britain, 21,90
 in United States, 21,90,91,92,93
Hunt, Robert, 9

Indecent exposure
 in British libraries, 28,31,37-38,40,44, 45,46,47,49,50
 in Canadian libraries, 65,66,70,73,76, 78,80,84
 in United States libraries, 97,101,104, 106,107
Institutional factors, of library crime
 in British libraries, 42-47
 in Canadian libraries, 72-74
 in United States libraries, 103-105
Interior protection
 general
  in British libraries, 119-120
  in Canadian libraries, 128
  in United States libraries, 134-135
 security checklist, 148-151

specific
  in British libraries, 120-121
  in Canadian libraries, 128-129
  in United States libraries, 135-136

Keayne, Robert, 9-10
Kenyon committee, 6

Larceny, 91
Legislation, for library crime prevention, 14-16
Librarians. *See also* Staff
  attitudes towards stolen books, 16
Libraries
  development, 5,7-8,9,10
  mercantile, 5
  parish, 5
  private, 5,8,9
  public. *See* Public libraries
  social, 10
  subscription, 5,8
Library hours. *See* Schedule
Library of Congress, 11-12
Library Services Act of 1956, 11
Library Services and Construction Act of 1964, 11
Locks, security. *See also* Storage rooms, locked
  in British libraries, 118
  in Canadian libraries, 126-127
  comparative patterns of use, 141
  in United States libraries, 132-133
Logan, James, 9

Mather, Cotton, 9
Motion detection systems, 119
Multiple point protection
  in British libraries, 121-123
  in Canadian libraries, 129-130
  in United States libraries, 136-137

National Commission on Libraries and Information Science, 11
National Library of Canada, 9

Nonbook resources. *See also* Audio-visual material; Equipment theft
  in British libraries, 34-35
  in Canadian libraries, 67-68

Obscene telephone calls
  to British libraries, 28,31,37-38,39,44, 45,46,49,50
  to Canadian libraries, 65,66,70,73,76, 78,80,87
  to United States libraries, 97,107
Offenders
  in Canada, 61-62
  in Great Britain, 22-23
  in United States, 93,94
Overdue materials, as stolen property, 16
Oxford University, 5

Patrons
  age, as crime correlate, 13,73-74
  assault on
    in British libraries, 28,31,40,44,46, 47,49,50
    in Canadian libraries, 65,66,70,72, 73,76,78,80
    in United States libraries, 97,102, 104,106,107
  changing needs of, 2
  number of, as library crime correlate
    in British libraries, 42-45
    in Canadian libraries, 72-73
    in United States libraries, 103-104
  problem behavior
    in British libraries, 37-40
    in Canadian libraries, 65,66,69-71, 73,74,76,78,80,81
    in United States libraries, 97, 100-103,104
  vandalised cars of
    outside British libraries, 28,31,32, 44,45,46,47,49,50
    outside Canadian libraries, 65,66, 73,76,77,79,80,82
    outside United States libraries, 97, 98,104,106,107
  verbal abuse of

in British libraries, 28,31,38-39,
44,46,49,50
in Canadian libraries, 65,66,69-70,
73,76,78,80
in United States libraries, 101,
104,106,107,108
Personal property theft
in British libraries, 28,31,36,44,45,
46,47,49,50,53,54
in Canadian libraries, 65,66,68,73,
76,77,80,82,85
in United States libraries, 97,106,107
Personal victimization
in British libraries, 41-42
in Canadian libraries, 71
in United States libraries, 112
Personnel. *See* Staff
Photoelectric alarms, 119
Police
attitudes towards library crime, 15
calls to
from British libraries, 53,54-55
from Canadian libraries, 85-86,87
from United States libraries, 110,
111-112
communication links with
by British libraries, 123
by Canadian libraries, 126,131
by United States libraries, 133,
138,139
patrol coverage by
of British libraries, 116-117,125
of Canadian libraries, 125-126
comparative patterns of, 141
of United States libraries, 132,133
Police station, proximity to library,
107-108
Property crime, 59,60,62,90-91
Property line protection
in British libraries, 116-118
in Canadian libraries, 125-126
definition, 116
security checklist, 147-149
in United States libraries, 132
Prosecution, of library crime perpetrators,
15-16
Protective devices, staff use of
in United States libraries, 112-113
Public attitudes

towards crime, 89
towards library crime, 16
towards violent crime, 20
Public libraries
American Library Association
standards, 11
crime in. *See* Crime, library
demographic changes affecting, 2
development, 5-12
in Canada, 7-9
in Great Britain, 5-7
in United States, 9-12
economic restrictions on, 1-2
first, 10
social changes affecting, 2
Public Libraries and Museum Act of
1964, 6

Rape, 90,91,92
Reference material, theft of
in British libraries, 28,31,34,44,45,
46,47,48,49,50
in Canadian libraries, 65,66,67,73,74,
76,77,79,80,82,84
in United States libraries, 97,99,103,
104,105,106,107,108
Research, funciton of, 3-5
Robbery, 22,91,92
Roberts Report, 6

Schedule
changes, as crime response
by British libraries, 53-54
by Canadian libraries, 84-85,87
by United States libraries, 110-111
as library crime risk factor, 13
Schools, proximity to library, 82,107-108
Scotland
general crime patterns, 19-20,21
library crime, 49-50
costs, 52,53,58
library security, 125
Screens, security
in British libraries, 119,125
in Canadian libraries, 126,127
comparative patterns of use, 141
in United States libraries, 133,134

Index

Security, 115-143
  in British libraries, 52,115-125,140, 141,142,143
  in Canadian libraries, 125-131,140, 141,142,143
  checklist, 145-152
  comparative patterns, 140-142
  entry point protection
    in British libraries, 118-119
    in Canadian libraries, 126-127
    in United States libraries, 132-134
  general interior protection
    in British libraries, 119-120
    in Canadian libraries, 128
    in United States libraries, 134-135
  information sources, 147
  multiple point protection
    in British libraries, 121-123
    in Canadian libraries, 129-130
    in United States libraries, 136-137
  overall patterns
    in British libraries, 124
    in Canadian libraries, 131
    in United States libraries, 138
  personnel security
    in British libraries, 123-124
    in Canadian libraries, 126,130-131
    in United States libraries, 133,137, 138
  property line protection
    in British libraries, 116-118
    in Canadian libraries, 125-126
    in United States libraries, 132
  specifc interior protection
    in British libraries, 120-121
    in Canadian libraries, 128-129
    in United States libraries, 135-136
  in Canadian libraries, 132-142,143
Security personnel
  in British libraries, 121,122-123
  in Canadian libraries, 126,129-130
  comparative patterns, 141,142
  plainclothes, 122,123,126,129,130, 133,139,141
  uniformed, 122-123,126,129-130,133, 136,141,142
  in United States libraries, 133,136,137, 139
Services, crime effects on
  in British libraries, 53,55
  in United States libraries, 112
Signalling devices, staff use
  in British libraries, 141
  in Canadian libraries, 126,131,141
  comparative patterns, 141
  in United States libraries, 133,137-138
Situational factors. *See* Community factors
Smoke detectors. *See also* Heat detectors
  in British libraries, 120,125
  in Canadian libraries, 126,128
  comparative patterns, 141,142
  in United States libraries, 133,134
Sonic alarms, 119
Staff
  assault on
    in British libraries, 28,31,40-41,44, 45,46,47,49,50
    in Canadian libraries, 65,66,70-71, 73,76,78,79,80
    in United States libraries, 97,102, 103-104,105,106,107
  cars, vandalism of
    outside Canadian libraries, 65,66, 73,76,77,80
    outside British libraries, 28,31,32, 49,50
    outside United States libraries, 97, 98,104,106,107
  crime impact
    on British libraries, 56
    on Canadian libraries, 86-87
    protective device use, 86
    on United States libraries, 110, 112-113
  crime prevention training, 13-14
    in British libraries, 56-57,123-124
    in Canadian libraries, 87,126, 130-131
    comparative patterns, 141
    in United States libraries, 110
  security procedures
    in British libraries, 122-123
    in Canadian libraries, 126,130-131
    checklist, 151-152
    in United States libraries, 133, 137-138
  signalling device use

in British libraries, 124
in Canadian libraries, 126,131
in United States libraries, 133, 137-138
size of, as library crime correlate
in British libraries, 47
in Canadian libraries, 74
in United States libraries, 104-105
verbal abuse of
in British libraries, 28,31,39,44, 45,46,48,49,50
in Canadian libraries, 65,66,70, 72,73,76,78,80,82,86,87
in United States libraries, 101,104, 106,107,108,109
Storage rooms, locked
in British libraries, 120,121,125
in Canadian libraries, 126,128
comparative patterns, 141
in United States libraries, 133,135,139

Theft
in British libraries, 28,31,33-37,44, 46,47,48,49,50,53,54
in Canada, 60
in Canadian libraries, 65,66,67-69,73, 76,77-78,79,80,81,82,84,85,86,87
in Great Britain, 19-20,22
reporting of, 21,33
in United States, 90,91,92
in United States libraries, 97,99-100, 103,104,105,106,107

Uniform Crime Reports, 89-94
United Kingdom. See Great Britain
United States
crime
offenders' characteristics, 93,94
patterns, 89-94
regional patterns, 92-93
victims' characteristics, 93
victimization surveys, 91
library crime, 94-113
community factors, 105-108
comparative analysis, 96-113
costs, 108-113
institutional factors, 103-105

problem patron behavior, 97, 100-103
theft, 97,99-100
vandalism, 96-99,104,105,106, 107,108
library security, 132-142,143
crime effects, 139-140
entry point protection, 132-134
general interior protection, 134-135
multiple point protection, 136-137
overall patterns, 138
personal security, 133,137-138
property line protection, 132
regional differences, 139
specific interior protection, 135-136
public library development, 9-12

Vandalism
in British libraries, 28,29-32,53,54,55
car damage, 28,31,32,44,45,46,47, 49,50
community factors, 48,49-50
equipment damage, 31-32,44,46,49, 50
inside library, 30,31,44,45,46,49,50
intentional book damage, 28,29-30, 31,43,44,46,49,50
outside library, 28,30,31,44,46,48, 49,50
in Canadian libraries, 64-67,72-73,74, 77,79,80,81,82,84,85,86
arson, 65,66,73,76,77,80,82
car damage, 65,66,73,76,77,79, 80,82
community factors, 76-77
equipment breakage, 65,66,73,74, 76,77,80,85
inside libraries, 64,65,66,72,73,76, 79,80,84,85
intentional book damage, 64,65,66, 72,73,74,76,79,80,81,82
outside library, 65-66,73,76,80,82
in United States libraries, 104,105, 107,108
arson, 97,98-99
car damage, 97,98
equipment damage, 97,98
inside library, 97,98,104,106,107

intentional book damage, 96-97
outside library, 97-98,104,106,107
Verbal abuse
  of patrons
    in British libraries, 28,31,38-39,44,
      46,49,50
    in Canadian libraries, 65,66,69-70,
      73,76,78,80
    in United States libraries, 101,104,
      106,107,108
  of staff
    in British libraries, 28,31,39,44,45,
      46,48,49,50
    in Canadian libraries, 65,66,70,72,
      73,76,78,80,82,86,87
    in United States libraries, 101,104,
      106,107,108,109
Victimization surveys. *See also* Crime,
    library
  crime underestimation and, 27-28

definition, 4-5
in United States, 91
Violent crime. *See also* specific crimes
  in Canada, 59-60,61,62
  in Great Britain, 20,21-23,20,21
    offenders' ages, 22-23
  public attitudes towards, 20
  in United States, 90,91

Wales
  crime patterns, 19,20,21
  library crime, 49,50
    costs, 52,53,58
  library security, 125
Windows, unbreakable. *See also* Screens,
    security
  in British libraries, 119
  in Canadian libraries, 126,127
  comparative patterns of use, 141
  in United States libraries, 133,134,139

For Product Safety Concerns and Information please contact our EU
representative GPSR@taylorandfrancis.com
Taylor & Francis Verlag GmbH, Kaufingerstraße 24, 80331 München, Germany

www.ingramcontent.com/pod-product-compliance
Lightning Source LLC
Chambersburg PA
CBHW052127300426
44116CB00010B/1808